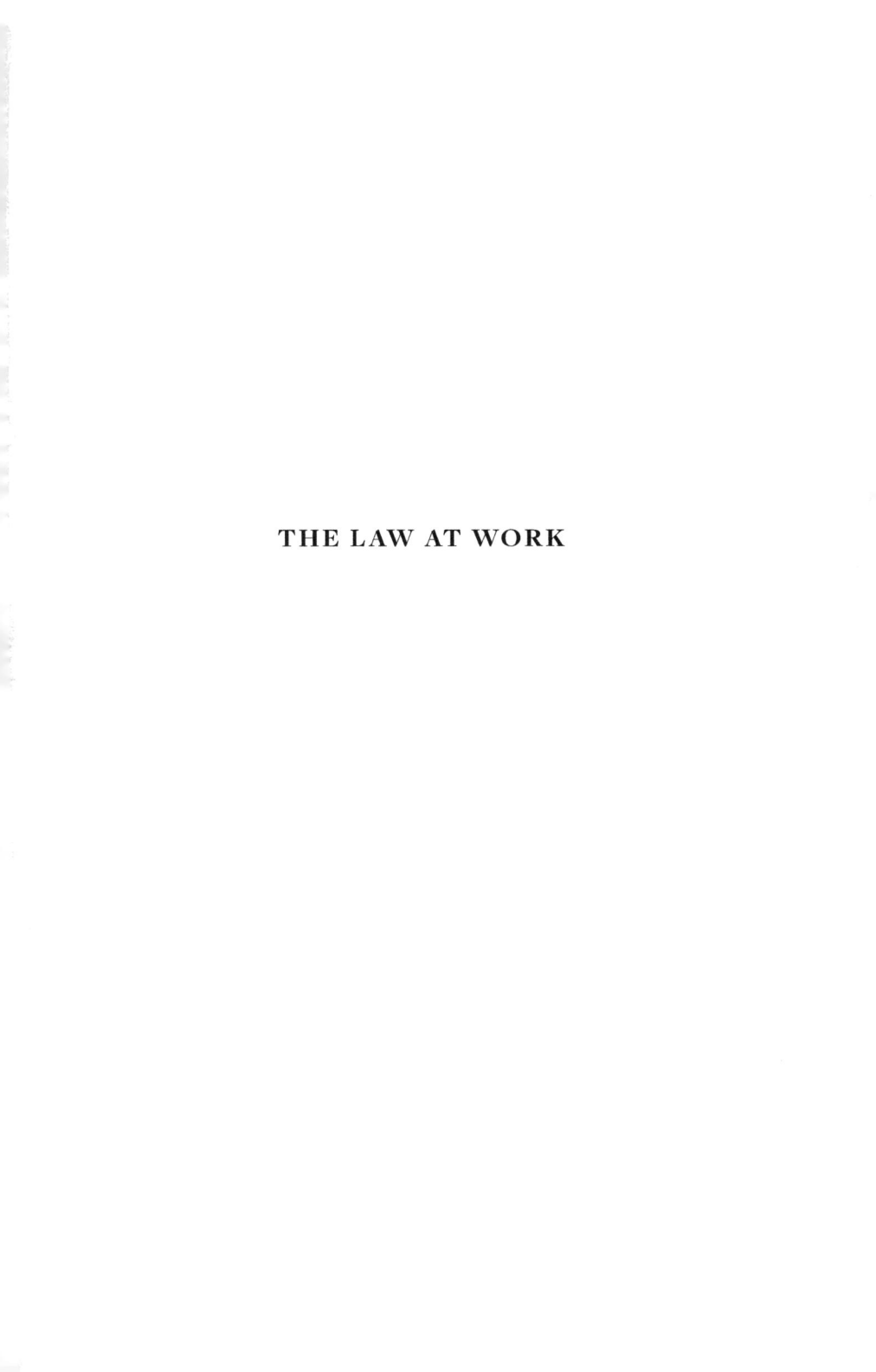

THE LAW AT WORK

The LAW at WORK

A Legal Playbook For Executives and Professionals

Alan G. Crone, Esq.

COPYRIGHT © 2023 ALAN G CRONE
All rights reserved.

THE LAW AT WORK
A Legal Playbook for Executives and Professionals
First Edition

ISBN	978-1-5445-3956-0	*Hardcover*
	978-1-5445-3955-3	*Paperback*
	978-1-5445-4005-4	*Ebook*

CONTENTS

Introduction   vii

1. Employment at Will   1
2. Negotiation, Compensation, and Terms   13
3. Intellectual Property   29
4. Electronic Data and Materials   43
5. Employee Discipline and Training   57
6. Office Politics   71
7. Discrimination   85
8. Hostile Work Environment   107
9. Whistleblowing   119
10. Exit Strategy   133
11. Non-Compete Agreements & Restrictive Covenants   147
12. Best Hiring Practices   163

About the Author   177
Acknowledgements   179

INTRODUCTION

Thanks for opening this book.

In my profession, every day is just that: an open book. I never know who's going to make an appointment and walk through our doors. They might bring with them any number of problems. Problems are my business—in my case, as an employment attorney, problems in the workplace.

For example, a few weeks ago, I found myself listening to a smart, sophisticated, and savvy woman we'll call Ashley. It was clear Ashley's problem had been weighing on her. She was the Chief Marketing Officer at a local business the owner/CEO was sexually harassing her. It started small on her first day at work, a suggestion here, a touch of the shoulder there, and it escalated from there. The CEO's conduct was only getting worse, and she was tempted to resign. But Ashley loved her job and didn't see why she should walk away.

"I'm tired of having this hanging over me," she said. "I haven't been eating much in the last few weeks. I find I can't sleep, and now I'm in regular therapy about anxiety, humiliation, and depression. It can't keep on like this. And before you ask me whether I've tried talking to the one harassing me, or reporting him up the line—well, he's the CEO. He's my boss. So that's out."

I nodded. "And the HR director reports to him, so that's out too," I said. "In small companies or at the very top there is rarely anyone internally to turn to for help. Often people think they have to suffer in silence."

Ashley was relieved I understood her predicament, "Exactly. There's no one in the company in a position to help me. We do have a company lawyer, and he happens to be my boss's personal attorney. I've had nowhere to turn until today."

My clients rarely have a resource at the company. HR, the lawyers, and management all work for the company, and ALL of them have the best interests of the company and the shareholders in mind, not employees' best interests.

I asked, "So what finally brought you to this office?"

"I have a friend from a networking group," Ashley said. "I told her my story, and she immediately suggested I talk to a lawyer. That was something I was reluctant to do because,

INTRODUCTION

well, I had the idea that it was something to do when you're trying to get a big financial settlement. And that's not me."

"It's not me, either," I said, "unless it's appropriate to a case."

Ashley said, "I did begin to think about getting a lawyer after my friend told me how it worked. I googled it, found your name, and called here for an appointment."

Most times when people come to see me, I'm the only professional they're consulting. They have friends and family, but that's it. Ashley was seeing her therapist, but usually, our clients have nowhere else to turn for professional guidance.

We talked for an hour and a half, and she filled in some of the details so I'd have a fuller picture. I previewed for her a few options for responding in the areas of discrimination and harassment. Two options were to escalate the matter with the Equal Employment Opportunity Commission or report it internally to HR. I described each of these including the pros and cons. Unfortunately, neither option is perfect. Standing up to harassment can be lonely and treacherous.

We didn't solve her problem in that session. But she seemed visibly relieved as she rose to leave after ninety minutes. I would hope she felt empowered, educated, and encouraged for the future.

I would never claim that lawyers have all the answers to every dilemma. The legal profession offers no miracle cure, but I've always had the experience that people feel better after speaking to a professional who understands the situation in which they find themselves—in this case, in the world of daily business. At the very least, they walk away with a clear understanding of their options and the ramifications of various choices they might make. Ashley was able to make an informed choice about how to report the harassment, and she was also armed with basic plans for what to do in case of various scenarios that could develop. Within a short period of time, her problem was solved.

I have more than three decades of experience in employment law, so I've had a great many conversations with employees, executives, and entrepreneurs of all kinds. I've been on either side of the toughest questions.

They come because they're having compensation issues, or because they're victims of discrimination. They come because they're the objects of retaliation, or perhaps it's because they're witnesses to something—illegal or unethical behavior in their work setting. And they're not certain how to report what they've seen or how to protect themselves from the consequences of these things.

Bad experiences at work can be frightening. Companies have more power than the people who work for them. And these companies tend to dominate our lives. Other than in marriage or with a significant other, the employment relationship is the most important we have. And in our culture, when

INTRODUCTION

we meet someone for the first time, we identify ourselves by where we work. Thus to a large extent, we are what we do. When a problem comes along with no apparent solution, it's no minor annoyance. We're in crisis, and we may have very little leverage to handle it. This is why I make the point that the very first service we provide in my profession is simply to listen compassionately, to reassure, and perhaps to relieve a bit of that gnawing uncertainty. This is someone in uncharted territory, and it's good to talk with someone who has a map.

For that very reason, after many years of these conversations, I began to realize that it might be helpful to place some of those more basic maps and descriptions in a book. I've brought together many of the most common scenarios and solutions for workplace situations for both company leaders and their employees.

By having this book handy, it might be possible for people to receive an early word on whether to go to court, to take some other action, or to take no action at all. Sometimes solutions can actually be rather simple; we just need to know the lay of the land. Other times, it might be valuable to realize from the beginning the issue is a complex and difficult one.

While it might seem obvious, I should mention that as handy and affordable as it may be, a book is no substitute for customized, thoughtful legal advice. Readers may decide they need to see an attorney about their problems, or perhaps a financial advisor or life coach. This book would then serve as a solid referral to seek professional consultation.

Either way, what I hope that you, the reader, may take away from this volume is the confidence that you don't have to live a daily life of doubt and worry. You're not alone with your crisis. There are ways to take charge of your work life and find resolution, so there's no need to feel hopeless or helpless. Expert solvers of every kind of problem are around, and assisting you is their mission.

I hope this book offers some measure of that expertise as well. May its pages shed a ray of light on your path ahead.

CHAPTER 1

EMPLOYMENT AT WILL

THE CITY OF CHATTANOOGA LIES ON THE EASTern end of my home state, Tennessee. It grew to prominence as a railroad center, with quick access to three states. The 1940's big band song "Chattanooga Choo Choo" captures that heritage. Transportation is good business.

L. Payne was a merchant there in 1883, and he had quite a problem. He filed a suit against the Western & Atlantic Railroad and asked the court for a remedy. Payne operated a prominent shop along Market Street from which he sold, among other things, a selection of whiskey.

Railroad employees would roll into the station from Atlanta and pick up a bottle or two from Payne's shop. Apparently, tipsy porters and brakemen became a problem for Western & Atlantic management, which decided to put a stop to the whole thing. W&A distributed a memo stating that any of its railroad workers who made any purchase from Payne's store would be immediately discharged.

Perhaps there was a better solution, but we'll never know. L. Payne lost a lot of business because of that memo, and he took the railroad company to court. His suit argued that its action unreasonably deprived him of business.

Did the railroad owe it to other businesses to provide its customers? The judge didn't see it that way. He dismissed the suit, and eventually the Tennessee Supreme Court upheld the decision, stating, "All may dismiss their employees at will… for good cause, for no cause, or even for cause morally wrong, without thereby being guilty of a legal wrong."[1]

The court also pointed out that employees enjoy the same right. Once hired, they can leave for any reason or no reason.

This decision, while a minor one in the great scheme of things, quickly became Tennessee's cornerstone case in the doctrine of employment at will—which, in turn, is one of the

---

1 Payne v. Railroad Company, 81 Tenn. 507 (1884), https://casetext.com/case/payne-v-railroad-company.

cornerstones of American employment law. The United State's Constitution and Laws offer protections of all kinds for common people, regardless of race, creed, or religion. We believe in basic fairness, and that may explain why so many Americans believe they have more rights in the workplace than they actually do. Basic example: an office worker is fired because the boss wants to give her job to an old school friend who has just moved to town. The discharged worker, her family, and her friends exclaim, "That's not fair! Can he really do that?"

Most of the time, the answer is yes, he can, fair or not. That's what the doctrine of employment at will is all about. Employers can hire or fire at any time, for any reason. They can treat their workers terribly, unless the action breaks a specific law.

Freedom and justice have always been cornerstone principles in the United States. The law at first, did not keep up with those notions in the early days of our Republic. Employment-At-Will was the law of the land without any exceptions until the late 1800's and early 1900's.

Just a little imagination helps us understand the necessity of this law. Think about a world in which workers could take their companies to court for any firing or perceived mistreatment. The judicial system would collapse under the weight of the resulting caseload. Practically any dismissal could result in a drawn-out lawsuit.

Of course, as the Tennessee Supreme Court pointed out, employees can come or go as they please too, unless bound by contract. The economic reality of America in the twenty-first century, though, is that many people don't have the luxury of walking away on grounds of the boss being a jerk or because their lunch break is too short. Good jobs are hard to come by.

The result is a workforce with very little "glue." Businesses can become revolving doors. The median span of an employee's time at one company is 4.1 years—a far cry from the time when your old granddad got that gold watch for forty years of service. Turnover rates are high, but in the twenty-first century, we do have a handful of exceptions to "easy-come, easy-go" employment policies.

THE BAD OLD DAYS

Employment at will didn't begin in Chattanooga; that case simply established the classic precedent for other cases. In truth, the concept has been in operation since medieval times, when lords ruled serfs to farm, fight, or care for the stables. He who had the gold, of course, made the rules. When there were disputes about how long an English common worker might be tied to working on one estate, the courts generally used one year as a reasonable term. As the early American colonies established their own courts, they adopted the British standards, including the one-year rule for indefinite agreements.

The sad concept of slavery established an extreme version of employment at will—the worker had no rights at all, including the right to walk away. That system, thankfully, was abolished, but employer/worker relationships weren't necessarily much better in the ensuing years.

The good news is that we've made progress. While the basic idea of employment at will continues, US Congress, state legislatures, and the courts have carved out exceptions to the doctrine over the last century and a half. In 1911, just a few decades after the railroad case in Chattanooga, a fire broke out at a shirt factory in New York City. The Triangle Shirtwaist Factory fire killed 146 workers, and it brought to public awareness the issue of sweatshop labor conditions—a common problem as the Industrial Age moved forward.

The shirt factory employed a great number of teenage girls who sat for long hours at sewing machines. The company could hire them for a few pennies an hour. They spoke little English. The proprietor had nailed shut all doors that led to the fire escapes because there was a problem with workers stepping out for a cigarette too frequently.

There were other issues, such as only one functioning elevator, that made it very difficult to move large numbers of people to the exits quickly. Manhattan still had quite a few wooden buildings in those days, and fires were a problem. When a flame quickly grew out of control, most of the workers were trapped inside and were killed.

This was also a time before safety inspections and Occupational Health and Safety Administration (OSHA) regulations—and though fires were frequent, there were few requirements in that area as well. Newspapers trumpeted the Triangle tragedy as a scandal brought about by heartless company owners, and the fire became one of the catalysts of the growing labor movement in this country. Collective bargaining helped produce safety regulations, child labor laws, and better conditions.

Later, in 1931, Congress got in on the act with the Davis-Bacon Act, guaranteeing fair wages; the Fair Labor Standards Act of 1938, establishing a minimum wage and overtime compensation; and age discrimination acts. All of these created exceptions to employment at will. Further allowances were established for citizens to serve jury duty and other basic responsibilities. In the 1960's, Title VII of the Civil Rights Act provided protection from discrimination and harassment based on sex, race, color, national origin, and religion. And more recently, the Family Medical Leave Act and the Americans with Disabilities Act have chipped away at employment at will a bit further.

As a result the American worker, be she an employee or executive, starts off as an at-will employee. The worker only has the rights the government gives her, or she can negotiate with her employer. Often people come to see me with a long list of complaints and grievances, and we have to carefully examine and analyze the facts and circumstances of their case to find, sometimes, an obscure basis for a claim, or at least leverage to negotiate better terms of a severance agreement. The exceptions—not the rule is where I live.

EXCEPTIONS

There are many exceptions to the employment-at-will doctrine. The most obvious and well-known exceptions are the civil rights laws. It is unlawful to terminate a worker because of her gender, age, race, national origin, or religious affiliation. Many states make it illegal to fire someone because she served on jury duty, because she filed a workers' compensation claim, or in retaliation for engaging in some sort of protected activity.

While exceptions exist for specific circumstances that workers commonly face, to date, there's still no law against being a bad boss. Nor, on the other hand, can one be sued for leaving a job position without giving notice. Most of us have been around businesses where somebody fails to show up one day and disappears. In those cases, the business has no legal remedy, because there's also no law against being a bad employee.

What's fair and what's moral are questions left for the workforce and its employers to hash out, but until good jobs are plentiful, the boss will continue to have most of the leverage. A worker with a complaint can gain legal remedy only if it perfectly fits an exception defined by the law. And specific, careful analysis is required to decide whether any particular case fits one of those exceptions. So there's a factual element, then a legal interpretative element, that must be put together to establish a cause of action against an employer.

What follows is a general list of points to consider for those who have potentially been victims of an unlawful employment action. Each case is different, of course. Details matter. If you have a specific concern, please contact an attorney.

- Are you in a protected class, such as age, gender, race, color, etc., that might provide you protection?

- Do you have an employment contract, or are you under a collective bargaining agreement? If not, the employment-at-will doctrine may be enforced under common law.

- As discussed, there are actually very few labor laws that protect you from a generic "wrongful termination" in employment-at-will situations. No matter how unfair you feel you may have been treated in a dismissal, there's no guarantee you have a cause of action. You must demonstrate that an unlawful action was taken.

- It's true that Delaware and the District of Columbia have adopted the Model Employment Termination Act (1991), which provides that employers have to show "good cause" for terminating an employee. Collective bargaining agreements (union contracts) may also contain "good and just cause" requirements. The reverse is not true, however; the employee may still quit for any or no reason.
    - "Good cause" or "just cause" are legal terms which mean that the employer must have a legitimate business reason for firing you.
    - Some examples of good cause include the following:
        - Wrongdoing on your part.
        - Gross negligence
        - Layoffs instituted to relieve the company during times of economic distress.
    - If you reside in a state that has adopted the Model Termination Act and you are fired, the court will consider some or all of the following to

determine whether your employer demonstrated good cause:
- Whether or not your employer made you aware of the policy you violated and warned you of the consequences in advance.
- Whether or not your employer gave you a chance to explain your side of the story.
- Whether or not the policy is frivolous. In other words, by violating the policy, did you really do anything wrong that hurt the company or other employees?
- How your employer has disciplined other employees for violation of the same or similar policies in the past.
- Whether or not your employer enacted the policy before or after you violated it.
- Whether or not violation of the policy is described as good cause for termination in an agreement, employee handbook, or similar document.
- Your employment record with the company.

A person may have a claim for wrongful termination if the *real reason* the company fired her is that she is a member of a protected category or engaged in protected activity. (We will examine both concepts in detail later.) If not, then she may have no recourse. The paradox is that she may never know the truth about the company's motivation.

EMPLOYER VS. INDIVIDUAL

This is a point to remember about employment at will. We think of it in terms of the great leverage it gives to employers, and the lack of protection against being unjustly dismissed. But the law is really about the company, not any individual who might happen to be the boss. It's still possible to have a claim against someone in the workplace, including the boss. That situation removes the action from the world of employment law, which is our concern here.

Imagine a woman working later hours who is sexually assaulted by a coworker. In that case, she may have both criminal and civil remedies against the individual, but she may or may not have a claim against the company. She could receive harsh treatment for taking action; she could be fired. She would point out that she was discharged because she filed suit against someone in the company. But that wouldn't necessarily translate into legal protection for her job. Legal relationships may become very complicated at this point. For example, the woman would be required in this situation to report the incident to the company, providing it an opportunity to handle the matter. Ultimately there could be business and personal issues entangled. In future chapters, we'll examine some of these problems.

Employment at will is a rather simple concept compared to many legal issues, though the details of a case could create some ambiguities. It doesn't head off unfairness in the workplace. Nothing is likely to do that, for as our parents told us many times when we were children, "the world isn't fair."

Just the same, we have more than two centuries of carefully and thoughtfully crafted laws to make sure the business world is as fair an environment as possible. We'll examine the most important areas in the chapters ahead.

CHAPTER 2

NEGOTIATION, COMPENSATION, AND TERMS

A VERY USEFUL TOOL TO AVOID THE NEGATIVE applications of the employment-at-will doctrine is to execute an employment contract. Such contracts can contain terms providing, for a specific term of guaranteed employment, exit provisions, non-competition or other restrictive agreements, benefits, compensation terms, and other provisions to allocate the risks associated with employment.

Let the buyer beware. You could end up selling your soul, just for ignoring the fine print. It happened to thousands of unsuspecting video game enthusiasts in 2010.

Gamestation, a store that sold computer games in the United Kingdom, added a clause to its online terms of service that year. It established that those who bought a game from the website henceforth agreed that the website owned their souls.

It happened to be April Fools' Day, of course, and the website manager was having a little fun with the concept that nobody reads the fine print. The clause stated:

> By placing an order via this web site on the first day of the fourth month of the year 2010 Anno Domini, you agree to grant us a non transferable option to claim, for now and forever more, your immortal soul.

In fairness, the store offered an opt-out provision. Just click the specified link, and buyers could retain possession of their eternal life force. The link led to a page with a congratulatory note for being a careful buyer, along with a voucher for five pounds of merchandise as a reward, presumably for good sportsmanship.

For a considerable period of time, no one complained since, in fact, no one read the fine print. Gamestation collected 7,500 souls before they decided to come clean, remove the clause, and forfeit sole rights to souls.

Most of us, of course, will be amused by that true story, then go right on ignoring fine print. There's simply too much of it in our lives. We use new computer software and phone apps with lengthy disclaimers, assertions, and requirements we're simply too busy to digest. When we purchase a home or a car, the "signing session" is long enough; if we took the time to pull out our magnifying glasses and read all those contracts line for line, we'd be there for weeks.

The law requires careful and comprehensive wording, and most of the time we simply trust that the vast majority of it is noncontroversial and is being offered in good faith. And usually that's the case. But there are occasions when we need to be much more vigilant. A recent example is the publicity given to "terms of service" contracts on the internet. Millions of people have signed away significant amounts of their privacy simply by creating an account with a social media site or some other online purveyor. Some of the larger internet companies are under fire for the stealthy collection of valuable customer data.

Accepting new employment is another example and the subject of this chapter. Employment contracts aren't always necessary, and in many cases aren't even used. But as employment relationships grow more complex in today's world, they're becoming more common, perhaps for the protection of both sides.

People often ask me to review an employment contract and ask, "Is this standard?"

My answer is always that "there is no such thing as standard." Each contract is different because each employment situation is different. Applying common or "standard" language to different fact situations might yield different legal outcomes.

In the most common scenario, a young lady, we'll say, is preparing to accept a new position and knows she'll be negotiating. She is handed a contract to review. She knows she wants the job. It represents a positive step in her career. She flips through the pages and notices she'll be initialing, dating, and signing various sections. There are lots of tiny details, but this isn't much of a concern. She intends to sign the contract and hope all goes well.

Many times—perhaps most—it does go well. The contract is basic and fair, and once she signs it and hands it to her new employer, the document goes into the file cabinet and no one looks at it again. But there are also cases when it does *not* go well. The job may not turn out to be a good fit. Some kind of issue could develop between employee and employer. She may want or need to leave, the company may want or need her to leave, and at some point, a dispute arises in which a legal remedy may be necessary. At that point, what's written

NEGOTIATION, COMPENSATION, AND TERMS

in all those contract clauses will matter tremendously. So it's important to review the entire contract carefully, or at least have someone well versed in employment law do so, before you apply your signature.

But what if you actually have no real leverage in terms of negotiation? In other words, what if it doesn't matter if you object to something, because the company is offering you a standard contract, take it or leave it? Even then, it's a good idea to have an attorney study your employment contract before you sign. As has been said many times, the devil is in the details. Understanding the meaning of certain terms and conditions might alter your desire to sign the contract.

ON LOOKING BEFORE LEAPING

We've all heard the stories of authors or musical artists who signed deceptive contracts and were deprived of their deserved financial royalties or film rights as a result. The 1950's singer Little Richard had a smash hit with the song "Tutti Frutti," and he was paid fifty dollars for all the rights to the song. Specialty Records, his label, owned the sound recording and the publishing rights, and Little Richard received half of one penny in royalty payments for each record sold. He had signed the contract, just happy to have one. Later, he told the press, "The only way I can [break] it is if I die or by an act of God."

Your contract is less likely to follow that model. But even when you believe your contract is fairly standard, it's highly recommended that you have an attorney review it before you sign.

For example, there might be a highly restrictive non-compete component in an employment agreement. With no termination-for-cause requirement in the contract, it could be a deal-breaker if you have a different understanding of the terms. For salespeople, for example, a non-compete clause would be a serious limitation to consider. In sales, someone's economic power is based on their accumulated knowledge in that field and in customer relationships. Perhaps they're willing to forfeit those, but they'd at least be wise to know what they're signing.

So even when you lack the opportunity to negotiate a contract, it's worth considering that there could be undesirable elements of the position that are hidden behind some of the technical and legal terminology. I also believe people tend to undersell their own negotiating power. Are you certain it's "take it or leave it"?

Better terms may still be available, and you'll never know without asking. The best time to negotiate is that moment of saying yes or no, before a contract is signed and you've become locked in.

"GOTCHA" CLAUSES

Let's consider a higher-level negotiation. A CEO has agreed upon a contract, but his concern is that he could work there for a few years, then get eased out. He might have seen this done to his predecessor. Maybe the company will be part of a merger, or maybe there will simply be a decision to go with someone younger. So he's concerned about his job security. He does see there's a prominent non-compete clause in the contract. So he has to consider the scenario of being forced out and having no place to go. He voices his concern.

The employer counters with the offer of a ten-year guarantee and a just-cause provision. That is, he can't be fired frivolously. The company would have to show strong cause, defined by gross misconduct, illegal activity, or some other true firing offense. The CEO feels he can rest easy with this agreement. He's not going to get arrested or involved in some scandal, and ten years is a nice period of time.

What he didn't notice, however, is that other provision tucked away in the agreement—the one that says either party can terminate this contract within ninety days. So theoretically, he doesn't have a ten-year contract; he has a ninety-day contract. That's drastically less security than he was looking for.

Yet as an attorney, I see such things all the time, in all kinds of contracts. The CEO could have pointed out the odd term and said, "I won't have a tenured contract if you leave that in." The lawyers who wrote the contract may have included it as an honest mistake, or it could be intentional. The reason doesn't matter, because it's a contract and is enforceable. "I didn't see that when I signed it" is rarely a good courtroom argument.

The contract may also be even more durable than it appears. At the end of an employment contract, you'll generally find a zipper clause. It says that every aspect of the agreement between the two named parties is contained in this contract; it zips up the whole issue, in other words.

So, later, the CEO might argue he was given this or that promise verbally, but it won't matter. He won't be allowed to bring in any other evidence if terms are clearly spelled out on paper. The judge will look at what's plainly written in the contract.

Notice the word *plainly* in the previous sentence. There could be a bit of wiggle room there. The judge will listen to other arguments if the wording is vague or ambiguous. If you have a vague or ambiguous contract, of course, you don't have a contract. This is another reason that, whichever side of the negotiation you're on, you'll want an attorney to read the contract carefully. You want to be sure the agreement allocates all your risks properly and provides certain rights.

There are also cases in which some of those risk allocations or other issues aren't covered in the contract. Sometimes business employers omit certain terms intentionally because they may not want to negotiate in that area, for whatever reason. The other side may have the same sentiment. Maybe there's no morals clause in the contract. This just means both sides lack a complete contract. Neither side is protected once that issue arises.

The previous chapter discussed employment at will. A written contract is a strong exception to that practice. If your contract specifies a guarantee of ten years' employment, the company is bound to that. Otherwise, no matter who you are, you can be terminated for any reason. For all these reasons, it makes sense to read every word of an employment contract.

COMMON CLAUSES

Here are a few common clauses to watch closely.

1. THE TERMINATION CLAUSE

It's important to pay attention to how either side can terminate an agreement. This is where the CEO learns what kind of tenure protection he's being offered. Is there a set guarantee, or could you be dismissed at any time? What kind of notice will you be given?

2. COMPENSATION TERMS

Obviously, this is where the eyes travel first for many executives who are negotiating. "What will I be paid, and how?" is a central issue for most of us. Pay attention to how compensation is calculated. Those in the field of sales will pay special attention because compensation can be in terms of guarantees and/or sales commissions. There may be an intricate arrangement, such as one year of guaranteed salary, then straight commission; it could be a more complex formula. It's wise to ask both an employment lawyer and a tax professional to review these details. The tax ramifications are going to matter, and in case your employment attorney isn't also knowledgeable in this area, you'd want to bring in someone who is.

Pay close attention to the language and its specificity because commissions can be calculated down to one or two key data points—contract price, net profit price, or some formula so convoluted that it's impossible for you to understand the deal you're being offered. When you see that kind of complicated formula, it's a red flag.

When does the commission vest? As soon as you earn it, or will you still be able to collect it if you're no longer with the company before it's due? Do you keep the commission at that point, or does the company retain it? Also, how tight is the compensation agreement? Can it be amended or changed at any time without your approval? All of these questions need to be considered for those paid by commission or some other non-fixed method.

3. JOB DUTIES AND RESPONSIBILITIES

Companies may or may not include this section spelling out the job description. If it's there, it's there for a reason. The employee will want to think carefully about the terms set forth here to make sure he or she agrees completely. Again, it's a mistake to think there's flexibility in a written contract because there was a verbal acknowledgment of such at the beginning of employment. Positions do grow and change. You want to make sure the contract acknowledges the possibility of normal shifts or reassignments that could happen over time. Particularly if you're highly compensated, this could become an issue down the road. Since job descriptions are flexible, take care with what's written in black and white on the contract.

4. ARBITRATION CLAUSES

Arbitration is an interesting substitute for due process. It's a way to resolve disputes apart from the time and expense of the judiciary courts. If you agree to arbitration, it will be enforceable except in certain specific circumstances. Arbitration law can be different in every state, but the federal act is extremely heavy-handed. It's also a contract item that may not be negotiable. The employer may insist on its inclusion in your agreement because most companies are eager to avoid long, drawn-out litigation.

Ask your attorney to review this area. You're agreeing to have any employment dispute, issue of discrimination, breach of employment, retaliation, or other problem arbitrated in private court rather than heard in the normal judicial process. An arbitrator, rather than a judge, would hear and rule on the case.

On the positive side, it's faster and less expensive. On the negative side, we get what we pay for. There's no jury of your peers or appeal process. You're bound to the decision of the arbitrator, who only needs to be sure he or she observes the law. If you want to present detailed evidence, you find that discovery is truncated, as is the number of depositions you can take and of documents you can request. It's a very condensed form of what would happen in a courthouse. So if your employer insists upon arbitration, you need to decide whether it's a deal-breaker.

5. JURY WAIVERS OR FORM SELECTION CLAUSES

Along the same lines as arbitration, this clause has to do with the company reserving the right, for example, to require that any dispute shall be governed by the laws of this particular state. The company may be based in Chicago, and you work from San Diego. Not only would this mean you'd have to travel, but you'd have to find an Illinois attorney to represent you. It may not seem like a huge issue during the excitement of signing an employment contract, but this clause could have huge ramifications later on. Just as in real estate "location" in litigation is terribly important. The location of your case could determine the laws the Court will apply, who the judge is, and whether the judge is elected or appointed. A distant forum can be very expensive as well.

You may not want a judge being the sole decider in your case. When you waive your right to a jury trial, it is gone. You will not be entitled to a jury to decide your case. A judge will decide. Is the company a large and important employer in the County? Is the CEO a large donor to the judge's campaign? Is the judge a former corporate lawyer or consumer protection lawyer? Does the judge have *any* employment law experience? You will not know the answer to most if not all of these questions until you file your lawsuit.

6. ATTORNEY FEE CLAUSES

These are what we call fee-shifting provisions in some agreements. They allow the prevailing party to recover attorney's fees from the other side. That is, if the company were to sue the employee for some reason, and it prevailed, the employee would foot the entire bill. This isn't a two-way street; in most cases, the company would be far more capable of paying lawyer fees and expenses than an individual. So signing off on this clause could have a tremendous chilling effect on whether the employee decided to contest some issue, receive pay that has been withheld, or something else.

You should also carefully examine the clause to see if it is reciprocal. Often such clauses only provide for fee shifting if the company wins. It is not unreasonable or unusual for an employee to negotiate a mutual prevailing party clause.

7. ZIPPER CLAUSES

We've already discussed these contract closers. The parties agree that all matters between them are covered in this agreement. It has the effect of cutting off any further reasoning or bargaining. As a zipper closes up something, this clause constitutes a waiver of the right to contest issues negotiated inside or outside the terms of a contract until its expiration.

8. RESTRICTIVE COVENANTS

A key issue for the employment relationship is whether an employee may leave the company, then compete against it, approach that company's customers, or make use of information obtained through employment there in a separate business. If there is a no-compete clause, the question is, for how long? What defines the information that can't be reused?

These can be controversial items. There are several types of restrictive covenants, all based upon those issues. Since this is a significant issue, we'll delve into it in a future chapter.

CONCLUSION

As we've acknowledged, most contracts aren't minefields full of traps for the unsuspecting. It's in the interest of companies to have happy, motivated employees who feel they're being fairly treated. The bulk of employment contracts are probably, to some extent, boilerplate in nature. Which isn't to say they should be quickly eyeballed and signed. Always read what you sign, and when there are terms and policies that aren't understandable, seek an explanation from an experienced attorney.

You may not be in danger of selling your soul, but think of it this way: you're selling the best hours of your life, week in and week out, to an employer. You might as well have a good idea of how that relationship is going to work.

Your best moment for leverage is *before* you sign. Many terms are negotiable depending on how badly the company wants to hire you. (What is your relative negotiating position?) It never hurts to test the boundaries of your leverage on key terms.

Many terms can be leveraged against others. For example, you might be able to negotiate a better termination provision in exchange for greater protections for the company in the restrictive covenants. You never know until you try.

Do not be afraid to walk-away from a position if the employment contract is too one sided. All the terms of employment are important. Don't assume that a bad term, like a non-compete clause, can be handled later. Once you sign it—you are stuck with it.

CHAPTER 3

INTELLECTUAL PROPERTY

HAVE YOU EVER HAD A REALLY STRONG, TRULY original idea? How could you be sure you owned that idea? Could someone else overhear your description of it at a cocktail party, then exploit the idea as their own? Of course they could.

Steve Jobs was offered a plant tour of the Xerox labs with his new Apple team, and as he walked through the work stations, he spotted a little hand device that moved the cursor on a computer screen. He took the idea, added some tweaks, and it became what we call the mouse. Xerox hadn't protected the idea. Later, Bill Gates did some software writing for Apple and used that work as the basis for his new Microsoft Windows software. "If they didn't want us to steal it, they should not have given it to us," Gates said later.

Intellectual property is an umbrella term that refers to original creations of the mind—in music, story, invented product, art, or anything else we might come up with on our own. This has become a very active and controversial area of the law. As another example, Mattel, the toy company behind the Barbie doll, won a large suit against another doll manufacturer, MGA Entertainment Inc., in 2008. MGA had introduced their Bratz line of dolls and was claiming that Mattel had introduced a similar large-headed doll that was undeniably similar to the Bratz doll.

But Mattel fought back, demonstrating that a Mattel designer had come up with the product, then defected to MGA with intellectual property already owned by Mattel. The judge and jury agreed. So MGA, which had brought the suit in the first place, was ordered to pay one hundred million dollars to Mattel and to take its dolls off the shelf.

We honor creativity in our country by protecting the rights of those who create. But intellectual property isn't always a simple matter. For example, if I show you the design of a cross, you would immediately think of Christianity. But that symbol, which is very simple, goes back many thousands of years. That's one reason no one can claim it as their own intellectual property.

What about one song that sounds like another? How close must it be to be classified as copyright infringement? Currently there's controversy over hip-hop songs that "sample" existing songs, using snippets of recordings. Are these little snippets intellectual property or not?

My grandfather's cousin had the wonderful name of Thomas Jefferson "Bozo" Williams. In 1923, he opened Bozo's Hot Pit Bar-B-Q along US Highway 78 in Tennessee, a well-known corridor somewhat in the vein of Route 66, and became known for some of the best Memphis-style barbecue around. He passed away in 1935, but his daughter Helen continued to operate the restaurant, and it thrived.

Some years later, Larry Harmon began investing his life into the character of Bozo the Clown, who had nothing to do with pulled pork or open pits. The character was invented for Capitol Records for children's recordings in the 1940's, and Harmon answered a casting call. But he saw his career destiny in the clown, and in 1957, he purchased the licensing rights for Bozo from Capitol and franchised local Bozo TV shows all across America and even overseas. Eventually there were Bozo toys and an animated cartoon—the clown had a red nose and a golden touch.

There were no barbecue-related conflicts until 1982, after Bozo Williams had passed away. Helen Williams wanted to open another restaurant on Beale Street in Memphis, and she sought to register the trademark. This brought the restaurant to Harmon's attention, and he filed suit to deprive her of the Bozo name. He argued that he'd bought that name and invested heavily in it. She argued that her father had been Bozo before Harmon was even born and had never made use of clowns or anything related to Harmon's property. Bozo was simply what folks called her dad, and that name had come to mean something in Western Tennessee. If Harmon had invested in the Bozo name, so had the Williamses.

The case worked its way through the system all the way to the United States Supreme Court. Harmon's best argument was this: the name now reflected on his product. If someone ate the pork sandwich and got acid indigestion, they might blame the clown. The barbecue lawyers countered that it was simpler than that: Harmon had only bought entertainment rights, not food service rights. And in fact, the Supreme Court found in favor of the restaurant. Bozo's Open Pit has been sold, but today, it's still a popular destination.

Meanwhile, the TV character, who was always billed as "the world's most famous clown," isn't so well known to today's children. Krusty the Clown, the satirical version of Bozo on

The Simpsons, is arguably more recognizable. Clown fame is fleeting, but a good, hot barbecue sandwich is unforgettable.

My cousin beat the clown. Bozo's Barbeque can still be found in Mason, Tennessee, on Highway 78. A testament to the power of intellectual property.

IP IN THE INTERNET AGE

When the Bozo case began, life and media were much simpler. It was easier to reason that a TV clown in Chicago was unlikely to be confused with a barbecue restaurant in Tennessee. Just a few years after the case got its ruling, however, the Information Age began to change the world of pop culture. Everything is on the internet, and the lines of division aren't quite so clear.

There are other issues that make intellectual property such a hotly contested issue. A few decades ago, it would have been quite a chore to smuggle thousands of pages of documents out of an office. In 1969, Daniel Ellsberg illicitly transported seven thousand pages of a report on the Vietnam War, later known as the Pentagon Papers, out of an office in Washington, DC. Over months of time, he had laboriously photocopied these pages one at a time, then carried them out of the building. Today, all that information could be quickly duplicated to a thumb drive. The internet also makes it far easier to hack and steal information. If identity theft is a problem, so is intellectual property theft.

Sometimes you might carry such information on your phone or portable storage without even realizing you have it or what its true value might be. We tend to identify intellectual property with brands, such as Bozo, or formulas, such as the secret recipe for Coca-Cola, or manufacturing processes. But almost anything can qualify. Whatever makes a business property valuable, whatever gives it a competitive advantage in the marketplace, is intellectual property if it can be established that this person or this corporation established ownership.

Therefore, along with the employment contracts discussed in the previous chapter, new employees might be given a non-disclosure agreement to sign. Or there may be an intellectual property policy and procedure agreement. It would establish which documents and properties the company considers to be proprietary and confidential—trade secrets, in other words. It's been my experience that many companies actually don't understand what it is that distinguishes them in the marketplace. But more of them are beginning to figure it out.

The employer has to be clear about what the intellectual property is. Whether it's a process, a product, or a customer relationship—whatever it is, it must be spelled out in writing. A company can't simply throw out a blanket requirement that an employee can't make use of anything from the company.

That would seem obvious, but quite often there's ambiguity created when there's a lack of specificity about what is and isn't protected. On many occasions I've asked an employer to tell me what confidential information the other party has, only to find the employer can't articulate it. He'll say, "Well, you know—just information that's ours. They should know it's confidential."

Again, judges look at what's written in a contract. Companies understand that they have intellectual property, and usually they know how valuable it is to their existence, but they simply don't take the time to detail it, protect it contractually, or train their people on how to protect the information.

So the company must show what it considers confidential, then it has to show active steps it has taken to ensure that confidentiality. In other words, was it put into writing? Was it reviewed with the employees so that they had a clear understanding of what had to stay inside the company walls? It won't work to say, "All of our documents and correspondence are protected." They're not, unless they're specifically established as such.

FORMS OF IP

If you were to see a blue star on a silver background, you'd immediately think of the Dallas Cowboys—at least if you're a football fan. A sign on the highway with a golden arch needs no words; drivers recognize the message that a McDonald's restaurant is at the next exit. Simple emblems, associated with specific colors, have strong associations for us, and we make buying decisions based upon them. It's intellectual property because a lot of time and investment has gone into establishing those brands, logos, and images.

Walt Disney has been well known for protecting its vast library of intellectual properties, spending millions of dollars to slow down the incessant borrowing of all those loveable characters. The company will send cease-and-desist orders to daycare facilities that have large paintings of Mickey Mouse and Donald Duck on the wall. The Disney argument is basically the same that Larry Harmon made on behalf of Bozo: if there's a bad experience at that daycare center, people will associate it with our characters.

Sometimes the property is less obvious. I have a preference for car rental companies. The company I consistently choose has established a reputation for doing everything better. The details of doing business with them are always superior, in my experience, and they set the standard for that business. What is it that separates them from their competitors? They have the same models of cars, the same availability at airports and other places. The difference is in the processes they've developed, the systems for delivering the right cars to their customers in a timely fashion and creating a positive experience. They're unlikely to share those processes with us, where competitors could take note. And I would hope their large numbers of employees are briefed on the confidentiality of those things, but they're the true value of that company.

For other companies, the key property is simply a mountain of data. Think of the value of what Facebook and Google have gathered on the public. This sounds unlikely, but it's been estimated that Google possesses two gigabytes of information on most people, or the equivalent of 1.5 million Word documents. Your browsing history, your purchasing history, where you've traveled, who your friends are, which topics are hot-button subjects for you, and countless other items are stored in databases and are virtually priceless to marketers and also political mavens. We'd rather they didn't have it, but that's neither here nor there. It's property they've spent billions of dollars collecting over time.

Internal data is another form of intellectual property. A manufacturing company produces rubber gaskets for automobile air filters. This is an ongoing product, and the company has put together data on how many gaskets can be produced by this kind of team on that kind of equipment; what the optimal speed of production should be; what the scrap rate for subpar product is; and so on. This isn't as creative as Mickey Mouse or the Nike swoosh; it isn't as profound as Big Tech's gathering of data. It happens in a factory setting where rubber rings are separated from rolls of material. But that's intellectual property all the same, because it has great value to the manufacturer. It allows for accurate and competitive pricing of those gaskets. How can we win this business contract with the lowest price, while still making a profit?

BEWARE OF AMBIGUITIES

All of these considerations go into what makes up intellectual property. It's also an added value for the employee, if he is being paid to maintain and guard intellectual property. The company places so much importance on it that caring for it is a more elite position in the company. And if you have that position, then leave the business, you expect to have a non-compete clause with which to abide, and the inconvenience of that should be reflected in your compensation.

This means that as you negotiate for a new position, you need to keep in mind what the intellectual property of that company is and what your relationship to it might be. What secrets will be entrusted to you? What is spelled out in the contract? What would be the implications for leaving the company, in terms of making use of the skills and product knowledge you've gained? In some cases, you might have learned how to operate that gasket press. That's not intellectual property in and of itself, so you could use what you

INTELLECTUAL PROPERTY

learned. But were there special processes and systems used that were unique to that company? And were you briefed on these? Are you contractually obligated in any way that would restrain you from making use of your experience?

Or imagine this scenario. You're a copywriter. A CEO hires you to write blogs, newspaper columns, letters, and other material for him. You sign a contract stating that all of these creative works will go out under the name of the CEO and that you're forfeiting all rights to them—which is fine, because all the material is on subjects of interest to the CEO's company and not to you. It's a good day job.

But at night, you write a novel. It's published, and it's a remarkable success. The CEO calls you into his office, congratulates you, and reminds you that he owns all your creative work. But you did it on your own time, of course. He says that doesn't matter—he's sure you must have planned much of it in your mind while on work hours. Clearly it's a terrible argument from the CEO's perspective, but it's possible it could still be a winning argument if your contract was written in a certain way. Did you forfeit all rights to your creative content for the span of the contract? Did it specify that the contract only applied to certain pieces written under the CEO's name? Were you an independent contractor, or work for hire?

Creative works are protected from the time they're created in a fixed form. If you write a poem or work out a song on guitar, it is yours as long as it's recorded on paper, software, audio, or some other permanent medium. When writers worried about their ideas being stolen, they were often told to type the story, seal it in an envelope, and mail it to themselves for the sake of the postmark. Then leave it sealed. This would establish a time frame.

Only the creator can claim copyright. But the exception is "works made for hire." In those cases, by agreement, the employment would assume copyright ownership. Writers often work under a work-for-hire agreement, but these, too, can become complicated. In recent years, independent publishing has become a large trend, with authors retaining all their rights rather than working through publishers; recording artists selling from their websites rather than record labels; and even comic-book artists forming publishing groups to own their own material.

Consider what is the most valuable asset your company possesses. It is most likely "how" it does something, not what it does. It could be the "brand." A solid brand will drive revenue, customers, and partners. All the work to build a brand can quickly be destroyed if the brand is not carefully nurtured and protected.

So these can be knotty issues. This chapter can't begin to cover all the issues of modern intellectual property law. Of all the chapters in this book, this may be the one that could be a book in itself. Until somebody writes that book, the best advice is once again to read that contract carefully, keep an eye out for issues of confidentiality, consult an attorney, and ask him or her good questions.

CHAPTER 4

ELECTRONIC DATA AND MATERIALS

H AVE YOU EVER NOTICED THE SAVE ICON IN computer programs as you create a document or spreadsheet? If you're below a certain age, you'd have no idea what it is. We still use the image of a computer diskette, straight out of the nineties, for Save. Those younger than thirty or so have probably never handled that little plastic diskette that held a whopping 1.44 megabytes.

As you can imagine, as the computing scene exploded thirty-plus years ago, our data outgrew those little disks very quickly. Those had succeeded the eight-inch floppy disk, which held about 80 kilobytes—eighteen times as small! Two or three simple documents, with no images, might fit on an old floppy.

Of course diskettes gave way to CD-ROM disks, which held an astounding (at the time) 670 megabytes. Those gave way to larger storage solutions, such as ZIP drives and finally, off-site cloud storage. As far as local use is concerned, most of us now use small dongles, known as thumb drives because that's about their size. But those might hold as much as a terabyte—one trillion bytes. We no longer even consider the vast reaches of our digital storage.

But let's try anyway. After all, it's still growing, and rapidly. The total amount of data we're creating, copying, and consuming each year is now projected to be 64 zettabytes. That's one billion terabytes, and think about what's in there: all the pictures from our cameras; all our spreadsheets and documents and tax statements and downloaded songs. During the pandemic, of course, we used even more of this digital information through home entertainment, teleconferences, and other digital media.

A great deal of that is impermanent and deleted, and it takes up very little physical space, considering what's contained. But the truth is that a great portion of our lives is now recorded in digital data, which is really nothing but far-flung

ELECTRONIC DATA AND MATERIALS

rows of ones and zeroes. Life has changed immeasurably in the past three decades.

This means that electronic data becomes a focal point of business and business law. Each day we're generating more data at work through email, memos, correspondence, client information, proprietary product information, and other material. We often use collaboration software that allows us to work together on documents and materials, and our phones are no less than small computers that carry all this with us, outside the office door and into the world. We spend all these hours laboring over numbers and words that exist on the internet. Just as huge financial transactions take place without any physical money changing hands, business transactions transpire globally and completely online.

So what happens when someone leaves a company in contentious circumstances, and she's suspected of taking important and confidential data with her? Some of it may simply be available on her phone, until her access is cut off. But she could very easily have used a small flash drive or some other means of taking information with her. She may have the full customer list and records of sales. She could have product secrets or other intellectual property. She could be holding incriminating memos. We've seen these scenarios play out in the headlines recently. There's tremendous power in the secrets found in electronic data.

PROTECTING DATA

I've found that the size of the company is largely irrelevant to its effectiveness in protecting its data. There are large companies with plenty of resources that have overlooked the necessity to shield the incredible value of their digital holdings. There are small or startup companies with tech-savvy leaders who handle and protect e-data well.

Any company needs to have a thorough and accurate accounting of all the electronic devices used by its employees. Furthermore, companies need to have strong policies on the use of electronic information, particularly pertaining to personal devices used for business purposes.

These days it's common for people to be issued smartphones by their companies. The same is true of laptop computers. And when these employees leave, they're often allowed to keep their phones or laptops. The company had better have a protocol for wiping all the proprietary information from these devices at the time of the employee's departure. If the company allows this person to walk away with this material on a phone or laptop, they might lose their protection over it. How valuable is a database of customer information, purchasing records, or other proprietary secrets? Priceless. Most of our ability to do business is in the information we hold, and most of that information is recorded in digital form.

ELECTRONIC DATA AND MATERIALS

So we shouldn't even have to state the fact that companies need policies for this kind of thing—it's obvious. The best-case scenario, and one that is becoming more and more unrealistic, is that there would be electronic devices for work, and others for personal use, and never the twain shall meet. All business would be transacted on business property that was collected on the final day of employment. But we know this is rare.

People frequently email themselves documents to work on at home. This simply increases the number of devices where this data exists. The information could leave the office through a cloud program, or it could be done with a flash drive. If this happens, it will be nearly impossible for the company to retrieve the information, if it even knows this happened. In most cases, the employee isn't trying to do anything nefarious; he's simply wanting to do a little extra work over the weekend.

Business policies should be created, and the employees trained, so that all company information remains in-house, if at all possible. It's clearly an uphill battle, and officers will need to be vigilant about enforcing this kind of policy. We've all become very casual about taking our data wherever we go.

Another issue often neglected is the electronic footprint we leave behind in our data traffic. Sometimes we work under the illusion that we're having secret conversations or secret web searches on company machines. Almost nothing is secretive in the modern age. Every keystroke, every download, every page visit leaves a footprint that a capable forensic systems expert can trace. We may feel we've deleted documents or cleared the cache of the web browser. But it's amazing what can be recovered.

Most of these things we already know. We simply don't think about the consequences of what we're doing. We begin to take for granted the vast power of the electronics we use, and we don't realize the responsibility that gives us. In the Information Age, companies need to provide constant education on the topic of information security. To a large extent, what is generated in the office needs to stay in the office. Otherwise, employees could be accused of nefarious activity even if their motives were entirely honest.

A CAUTIONARY TALE

I worked with a salesman for an international merchandising organization. The company exported and imported goods all over the world, and he was an excellent salesman. We'll call him Nelson. He'd been brought in to develop a new market for this company—which we'll call XYZ Inc.—and he was successful in creating and thriving in that market.

Nelson was working under a complex commission structure. Different product lines were assigned different commission schedules. It could be very confusing just to calculate how he was doing for the month. So he kept a spreadsheet on his company computer. It turned out, during a particularly impressive year of work, that the complex commission structure worked in his favor, because he exceeded the sales quota consistently and was therefore open to large bonuses.

No one in management particularly noticed until Nelson had an amazingly fruitful year near the end of the per annum pay period, and then it became obvious: Nelson's commission was far beyond anything anyone could have imagined when he was hired. C-suite was taken completely off guard. It wasn't even clear whether the company could afford to make that commission-plus-bonus payment. It was well into six figures during what was otherwise a challenging year.

Nelson began to pick up on a bit of static from management—odd looks, subject quickly changed—that suggested his huge payout wasn't a done deal. The structure had been poorly written, and it would need to be reworked first. That was the direction this thing was heading, he suspected.

Nelson let management know that he wasn't going to sit still for that. A deal was a deal, he'd worked very hard, and he expected XYZ to honor its word. Then he began to think about where the policy in question had been written down, and where and how his sales were recorded, and whether any of that information could be altered or deleted. He began emailing documents to his personal Gmail account, including spreadsheets that would become evidence in case of litigation. Remember, the company's system was quite complicated, and he knew he could never recreate it from memory.

And it was becoming crystal clear to him that litigation was where this thing was heading. The payout in question was large enough to fight for, and the company was becoming more insistent about the fact that it would rework the structure, then pay him based on the new deal, as if that were fair.

The relationship between the two parties became strained and awkward. Finally it came to a head. The time came, and Nelson asked, "Are you going to write that check?" The CEO said no, that wasn't going to happen. Nelson said, "Well, we'll see about that," and he turned in his resignation, hired a lawyer, and gathered all his evidence as he prepared to make a claim.

Meanwhile, given the acrimonious state of the relationship, XYZ's legal department conducted a forensic computer investigation. He had been emailing himself information, they discovered, and had downloaded materials onto a thumb drive and from there onto a hard drive he'd been provided. The company hadn't thought to retrieve that hard drive.

He had a lot of confidential information on his hands, and he was angry. The company feared he could use all this information against his old company in a variety of ways—give it to a competitor, hand it to the government, or set himself up to compete with the company in some way. So XYZ struck first, filing an injunction against him on the basis that he had stolen confidential and proprietary information from the company.

Somehow, there needed to be a fair reckoning of how much was confidential or proprietary and how much was not, and whether these documents were covered by the Trade Secrets Protection Act.

The contents of one of the salesman's thumb drives were downloaded to another machine that couldn't be located. He also had a home computer he shared with his spouse, who was a psychiatrist. Therefore confidential patient information was also caught up in this investigation. So there were all kinds of problems. Having clearly taken information while being unable to reproduce the media, he was in a difficult situation. It probably cost him more to defend this suit than he'd have made on the commission.

As with many lawsuits filed in anger's wake, he now had second thoughts about the whole thing. But the truth was that he hadn't thought about the ramifications of what he was doing. He had moved some numbers from one machine to another. He had transferred some documents so he'd have records of them. All of it concerned his own work and the company to which he still belonged when he made the transfers. These things don't feel like stealing—how could stealing be so easy and convenient?

WISER STRATEGIES

He'd been trying to "protect" certain data that he'd need as evidence. But if only he hadn't copied and transferred the data, there were strategies he could have employed, with good legal guidance, to ensure the company didn't erase those figures. From an adversarial standpoint, it's almost better to go ahead and let the company destroy the data because then, the court will presume it's spoliation of evidence. This is the other party's act of deliberately, negligently, or accidentally destroying relevant evidence. If the company had destroyed data, the court would have had a presumption that would have helped the salesman's case—just another indicator that he should have found a good attorney before acting on his own, with his lack of understanding of what his actions would produce.

I'll add that the above point doesn't hold true every single time. When there's enough money involved, and the company is powerful enough, it might actually have the ability to make evidence disappear in a way that doesn't look like spoliation. It's happened before, but in most cases, companies are flirting with disaster when they destroy evidence.

ELECTRONIC DATA AND MATERIALS

We instruct clients to make a list of the important documents and bring it with them—not copies of the document, just an inventory of what they are. Later, in discovery, the clients can request those documents. In some cases, when clients were worried about documents going into the shredder, we've suggested making a physical copy of everything relevant, putting it in a box, and hiding it on the premises. Then, in discovery, they can identify the markings of the box and ask for it to be produced. This would obviously involve copying, but not removing data from the site.

Of course, rather than worrying about a large box of files and how to hide it under some loose floorboard that's unlikely to exist, a better solution could be simply to place copies on the thumb drive, and hide it in an obscure file in the cabinet used a number of years ago, or some other unlikely location. Take pictures not of the documents but of the hiding place, and make sure the pictures are timestamped.

Or simply place the thumb drive in a sealed envelope and hand it to your attorney, in anticipation of litigation. You don't have access to it; your lawyer does, and can produce it at the right time. I don't recommend this way often, because you're still removing the documents from the workplace. But at least you could prove you were without access to those documents and that they weren't downloaded to another device.

In the cautionary tale above, what's important to note is that both sides acted without the benefits of preparation and understanding. The company had done no training with employees. It had communicated nothing about safeguarding confidential information. It gave out personal devices or encouraged the use of them without having a policy to guard against them being misused. Then, when the salesman resigned, in what was obviously a contentious scenario, the company failed to collect the devices, including a hard drive bought for him as a convenience.

Nor did the company instruct the salesman that the devices, particularly the hard drive, were only for company use. In time, as often happens, the hard drive began to feel like a personal belonging. He never thought to "steal" it; he simply forgot about it when he was returning his other devices. His personal things, and those of his spouse, were on that drive. The business data belonged to the company; it had a right to expect the information not to seep out of the company. But the onus was and is on the company to safeguard it.

If the company had a policy that employees must work on company provided equipment only, and can't email data to outside email accounts or devices, then this case might have come out quite differently. In fact, the company had no such policies and did not train employees on the proper handling of e-data. If it did properly protect its data and devices

ELECTRONIC DATA AND MATERIALS

perhaps my client would never have done anything to raise this issue.

The best advice from the corporate perspective is to stay on top of developments in the digital world and have at least a basic understanding of how things work there. When companies and individuals begin to move to new kinds of devices and computing, including cloud storage, pay attention. Ask your IT professionals to help keep you abreast of the ways your information is stored, how often it's backed up, and what access employees have to it. And again, we need to educate our employees about safeguarding company information.

We've indeed moved from floppy disks to backup drives to cloud storage, so there's no limit to the amount of information out there somewhere on servers, even as that information is our company's greatest asset. Simply be sure the security is strong. We see more and more cases of high-scale hacking and compromise of even some of the larger companies. Those of us in the legal profession know how private and how protected our digital information must remain. But it's also true that services such as Dropbox, Microsoft OneDrive, and Apple iCloud have outstanding security. The integrity of the security is worth billions of dollars to them. There was a time when I resisted uploading information to a "cloud," and I'd recommend a secure local area network on premises. But times have changed. There's little chance that anything we could host would match the security of the massive storage companies online. Just be certain it's a reputable, respected service.

For now, we have a good understanding of data security. But it's your job and mine to keep up with technology. Our lives and work are far too dependent upon it these days to do otherwise.

When an employee who has access to sensitive data departs a company the employee and the company should take immediate steps to make sure that all of the data and devices are secure and not "out in the open." Cases which involve the alleged mishandling of sensitive data can be crippling financially for both sides. The costs associated with discovery and preservation in these types of cases are often enormous. Employees who are proved to have taken such data lose credibility with the Court and jury. These issues can distract from other important issues such as: breach of contract; wrongful termination; enforceability of restrictive covenants; and, other claims.

CHAPTER 5

EMPLOYEE DISCIPLINE AND TRAINING

OUR SIMPLEST WORD PICTURE TO DESCRIBE leadership strategy is the metaphor of the carrot and the stick. It comes from an old French saying that describes the coaxing of donkeys. You dangle the carrot as a motivation to move, the stick as a threat when it refuses. It's the choice between positive and negative reinforcement.

We've all known a few carrot-danglers as well as some stick-wavers. But the stick is all but outmoded these days.

People don't respond well to donkey discipline. Perhaps they never did. But it wasn't really too long ago that employers could get away with heavy-handed leadership. If you wanted to work in that company, there were rules, and you could abide by them or you could walk. You followed a rigorous dress code. You maintained very high performance standards. There was absolutely no suggestion box. And discipline could be very strict.

During the past few years, TV viewers have gotten a picture of the bygone workplace through the series *Mad Men*, set in the early 1960s. Companies had all the leverage. Employees were simply interchangeable parts. And yes, Employment by Will is still a powerful standard. It's true that firing—in most cases—can happen for reasons just or unjust.

But during these times, we do still expect reasonable policies for company discipline. Early in my law career, I witnessed a fascinating case study along these lines. I was an assistant county attorney in those days. I represented a public official we'll call Adam, who decided to enter political life by running for an open seat. Adam was the outsider, while his opponent, Anne, was an established team member in the office that was up for election.

Adam won the election, and now he had to adapt to a brand-new kind of work. But the arrangement was awkward for another reason: Anne, his political opponent, was still present.

EMPLOYEE DISCIPLINE AND TRAINING

The two of them would have to find a way to work together because Anne had civil service tenure; her job was secure. Adam understood that even if the chemistry was terrible, Anne could not be discharged apart from special circumstances.

Adam was idealistic. He had ideas how this office would be run, and he began to change all the old policies. Anne was appalled by his wrecking-crew approach to so many procedures and structures she'd been a part of building. Who was this rookie, this newcomer, to walk through the door and begin changing everything before he even had any experience?

Anne believed she knew a lot more about these things than her boss, and for good reason. But when she tried to point out why his changes weren't the best ideas, he wouldn't listen. After a certain point, she began ignoring his many requests to change this or that. Adam decided he had no choice but to begin disciplining her. But how do you discipline someone with a protected position? One thing he knew was that in any case of discipline, every detail, every conversation, needed to be carefully documented.

Adam had a chief administrative officer who carried out all his instructions, and the two of them created a procedure to place Anne through progressive discipline, starting with a verbal warning, then a first written warning, and so on. Their plan was very detailed. The discipline would accelerate unless Anne got with the program. It would all be documented, and if her behavior reached a certain point, she would then be dismissed for cause. The officer crossed every t and dotted every i in recording the disciplinary steps. And right on schedule, Anne received her pink slip with receipts showing her violations. Based on the conditions set forth, it was an open and shut case.

Anne immediately filed a lawsuit for wrongful termination. At the hearing, her representative stood to make his client's case, placing into evidence all the progressive disciplinary documents that had been issued. They were neatly contained in three white notebooks. The question was whether they represented due process, offering reasonable opportunities for the employee to improve.

The attorney made his case that these memos and records showed no such thing. His theory was that the employee was targeted and the tenor of the documents indicated that the Employer was documenting to support a termination, not obtain improved performance. The jury reviewed the evidence and agreed it was clear these notebooks showed a premeditated path toward dismissal from the first memorandum.

DISCIPLINE VS. PUNISHMENT

Juries are smarter than some people expect. They understand human nature, and they tend to see through the camouflage that hides true motives. The jury in this case understood the white notebooks. They believed good managers should acclimate employees, giving them every chance to enjoy success. The purpose of legitimate discipline is growth, not punishment. If the employee really has no desire to be successful and isn't willing to cooperate, that's one thing. But discipline should be a bridge to advancement rather than an obstacle course aimed at the exit. The jury understood the awkwardness of the office situation but felt Adam was simply looking to fire Anne.

There was a time when Adam might have prevailed in court, for any number of reasons. Today, it's not simply a matter of the law. Companies with rigid disciplinary policies are far less likely to succeed than they were a generation ago. It's also true that good employees are not interchangeable parts; they're a precious resource. There's actually competition for the brightest and most skilled ones. It's also true that young people entering the marketplace are pickier about which career suits them. People look for a company culture that is progressive and positive. For millennials, quality of life is more important than mere salary size.[2] It's been demonstrated that the companies with the friendliest and most inviting cultures are the ones who end up outperforming their competitors.

---

2   Ryan Jenkins, "This Is Why Millenials Care So Much about Work–Life Balance," *Inc.*, January 8, 2018, https://www.inc.com/ryan-jenkins/this-is-what-millennials-value-most-in-a-job-why.html.

My advice to business clients is to pay attention to this trend. We need to move from discipline policies to employee training programs—from stick to carrot. The mindset has to be about empowering employee success and development rather than exercising control and authority over the people in our office. The day of simply demanding compliance is over if we want to have an effective business and a productive atmosphere. So our energy should go into shaping a dynamic, team-oriented culture rather than devising penalties as deterrence policies.

There's no shortage of literature out there concerning corporate culture-building. I certainly can't examine the various angles of that in a short chapter, nor is that my area of expertise. But I believe a strong and positive culture is built through beginning with an understanding of what it takes to be successful in your organization and what the company's expectations are. Then, as we've discussed in other chapters, we need to overcommunicate those ideas to employees. People are far less likely to internalize messages until they hear those messages a number of times.

We need to look at values and character when hiring, rather than simply skills and capability, and build our organizations based on people who are already culture compliant with the business we already have. Before new employees even come to work for us, it should be clear that they've embraced the spirit of the company we're building.

CLARIFYING PRIORITIES

What we're talking about, of course, requires a tremendous amount of proactivity with our business. It's not a matter of instituting a program or emphasis, but of building something from the foundation. It can't be done quickly, but once this culture is well established, it can create a vastly improved atmosphere around the office.

I've often said that the best way to avoid a wrongful firing suit is never to fire anybody. That might sound rather flippant, but consider the costs of running a business today. There are expenses of time and money that go into hiring, and more expenses of time and money that go into training. Constant employee transition is far more expensive than we tend to think it is. One study estimates that employee turnover costs businesses one trillion dollars per year in the United States. The cost of replacing an individual employee could range from half to twice the employee's annual salary.[3] That kind of outlay is saved by hiring the right kind of people into the right corporate culture. Firings decrease. Longevity and experience among the employees increase. And perhaps there's never expensive litigation.

---

3   Shane McFeely and Ben Wigert, "This Fixable Problem Cost U.S. Businesses $1 Trillion," Gallup, March 13, 2019, https://www.gallup.com/workplace/247391/fixable-problem-costs-businesses-trillion.aspx.

The most important guideline, however, is for leaders to have it straight in their own minds what is acceptable and nonnegotiable, to know what is expected from your employees, and to communicate that explicitly to them from the first interview. This way, people are more likely to "fire" themselves—before hiring—if they're not a good fit. That is, you speak seriously about your requirements during the job interview, and applicants are more likely to step away if they understand the mismatch.

It doesn't really matter what your nonnegotiables are. It could be arriving and starting work by 8:00 a.m. If that's imperative for management, it needs to be expressed, lived out, and repeated frequently. Applicants know if that's going to be a problem, so discipline is better handled through preventive maintenance than by struggling with what to do about it after the fact. If there's zero tolerance for profane language, eating at the desk, or personal phone calls and internet usage, then simply explain these things, write them down, and verbally reinforce the policy.

That seems simple, but in most cases, companies hire on proficiency and fire on behavior. In other words, Candidate A can type one hundred words per minute, and is hired instead of Candidate B, who types eighty but has a better attitude and who better fits the personnel requirements of the company. The twenty extra words per minute won't matter if that person raises disciplinary issues.

EMPLOYEE DISCIPLINE AND TRAINING

This is why companies are beginning to hire more on character and culture considerations, even if certain areas of proficiency must be trained. It works out better in the long run. Obviously, there are items requiring high competency in which we can be less selective; your IT professionals need to be excellent at their technical work. But all things being equal, culture should guide our team-building.

In the past, we've had codes of discipline. Instead, we need better training to accomplish the same purpose, and a system to work for the success of employees. That system is built around defining and stimulating progress rather than documenting failure. And again, such a positive message at the beginning of employment is going to be well received by everyone who is hired. Instead of "Here's why we might fire you," your message is "Here's how we'll help you become better at work and in life."

This isn't a matter of touchy-feely softness. It's good business. Every company should measure the personnel turnover in its office and compare it with the rest of the industry. That's a leading indicator of the effectiveness of your in-house culture. Which departments are revolving doors, and why? What programs and incentives have you developed to help people measure success, then move in that direction?

MAKING IT PERSONAL

If we're not going to manage by memo, but work through programs, goals, and healthy relationships—how do we handle the negative situations that still may arise?

For one thing, we need to restore the lost art of healthy confrontation. Many people simply don't know how to resolve conflict in a positive way today, but it can be done. Again, bringing in the right kind of people helps. What doesn't help, however, is avoiding confrontation, as many of us do, and hoping the problem goes away or waiting for things to come to some kind of head. Then there's usually unhealthy confrontation, and nobody enjoys that.

Nonconfrontational communication can solve most problems. Much of the time, we haven't even talked with people about what should or shouldn't be done.

A few years ago, a sixty-five-year-old former custodian came to my office. We'll call him Charles. The first words from his mouth were "I was fired because I'm an old Black man."

If he was right, there were two issues that were grounds for a discriminations suit: age and gender. Of course, I needed to know more about the situation. I asked him, "Why do you feel those were the reasons you were dismissed?"

"I got this new supervisor, a young white man," he began.

"Okay."

EMPLOYEE DISCIPLINE AND TRAINING

"And he was just on me constantly for every little thing. I couldn't do anything that met with his approval. So finally he fired me."

It certainly sounded like an unfair situation. But was it age or gender discrimination? We talked a little more in depth, and I finally pieced together what really got Charles in trouble: he was regularly about fifteen minutes late, and it drove his supervisor crazy. But Charles added, "I'd been coming in fifteen minutes late for twenty years on this job, and no one ever said anything to me about it." He had some mobility issues, and he didn't own a car. So for years, he'd been taking a bus to work. And he was limited to the schedule and regularity of that bus.

For the past supervisor, that was an acceptable factor. As long as Charles came in and got the job done, the precise hours weren't an issue. But for a new manager, timeliness was a much higher priority. So Charles was fired for chronic tardiness. Still, he said, "Suddenly I'm fired for being late, coming in at the same time as ever? You can't tell me it's not because I'm an old Black man." The two men were looking at the situation from completely different vantages.

He'd been warned to come in on time, but not clearly enough for the message to get through—because for him, this was the same job where his schedule had always been acceptable. But the new manager had different priorities than the old one. I could see that if he'd sat down with him, listened, and learned about Charles's hours and his transportation, then either they could have come to some accommodation to help Charles stay, or they could have helped him find another job closer to his home. But I learned that no such conversation ever took place. The new manager just came in and laid down the law. Healthy confrontation would have, at the very least, saved attorney fees and court costs.

Perhaps the new supervisor did want new blood in the job. Even in that case, he still owed it to a twenty-year employee to have a productive discussion about the situation. And he owed it to anyone in his department to know what the non-negotiables were. In the old system, arrival time wasn't one of them; in the new system, it was.

This is a classic story showing why we must have clear and complete communication. But that's harder than it should be for many people in the business world. We take too much understanding for granted, and we falsely assume saying something once or putting it in a memo is sufficient.

Good, accurate job descriptions are a part of this too. What happens when we hire people and offer perhaps a vague description of the required work but forget to mention some of the functions? What happens when jobs evolve and change over time so that someone is doing something completely different than they were hired to do? Management isn't possible when there aren't even written parameters.

EMPLOYEE DISCIPLINE AND TRAINING

Many companies revisit their job descriptions every five or ten years, and naturally they find the responsibilities have evolved and must be updated. But this should actually be done on a quarterly, or at the very least, a yearly basis so the company can find out what people are actually doing. Is the arrangement efficient? Is the workforce divided out properly for the various functions so that the right number of people have the right number of responsibilities?

And the more management levels between a job and the decision maker, the less likely it is that the decision maker will understand the job description. Many business leaders have no idea what happens a level or two beneath their place in the hierarchy, yet they make the important decisions for those levels.

So discipline should really begin with creation of the position because at that point, there's the most clarity about the job. The manager can decide what the expectations will be and can explain them to the jobholder. It takes a great amount of time, attention, and resources to understand the work at that level, but there's a strong benefit in company culture when the leaders do have clear comprehension.

A few decades ago, in a book called *In Search of Excellence: Lessons from America's Best-Run Companies,* authors Peters and Waterman popularized a phrase traced back to Hewlett-Packard: management by walking around. The idea was that strong leaders regularly wander through the company without any particular agenda, just observing how things are done and chatting with employees. Again, it's good for company culture and educational for the leader.

Those companies that build the most dynamic, positive cultures don't spend a lot of time writing memos about discipline. The issue simply doesn't come up as often, because they're proactive in their hiring practices, clear in their communications, and consistent in letting people know what is expected. As a result, the turnover level plummets.

Can you imagine if all our companies were run this way? I might be forced to find some other line of work.

CHAPTER 6

OFFICE POLITICS

E D WAS AN EXPERIENCED WAREHOUSE MANAGER at a manufacturing company. He reported to the chief operating officer, and for nearly twenty years, they had a good relationship. Then the COO retired. The CEO felt this was a good time to refresh the playing field and try some new approaches. He brought in JT, a man he'd worked with previously who had told him about some compelling strategies that had worked well for him.

Ed watched these events nervously. He wasn't thrilled about the idea of reporting to a new boss, and sure enough, he and JT clashed within a few weeks of the change. Ed had strong ideas about how to run his warehouse, and he'd developed them over all his years of experience at this company. Worse, JT actually had it in mind to bring in an executive from his old team and place him in Ed's position. That would take care of all the static Ed was creating.

So he began to stress-test Ed, putting him in various situations that required managerial choices, and seeing if he would respond in the way JT wanted. If not, then that would provide grounds for what he wanted to do—bring in his friend. JT would write up Ed, the warehouse manager, in preparation for eventually firing or transferring him.

Ed knew what was going on and he was upset, of course. He told his wife, his family, and his friends about his past achievements with the company, the smooth record of production, the quality milestones his warehouse had established, and how now, this interloper wanted to come in and force change right off the bat, without getting to know how things worked in this company.

Everyone close to him fully agreed with his take: this was an outrage, and he needed to fight back! Those who love us are always cheerleaders for our cause.

Ed came to see me, but sadly, I wasn't able to endorse his views as well as his friends and family did. The company and its management, I said, were well within their rights to make these changes. Such moves are very common in American business life. Even so, I encouraged Ed to ask important questions. Was there a safety issue in these new guidelines? Were OSHA regulations being violated in some way? Was there any technical case to be made that the new requirements were dangerous or unethical?

If not, there was really nothing Ed could do other than taking a deep breath, saying, "Yes sir," and getting back to work. Ed's disappointment showed on his face, but he knew this was the truth he'd been avoiding. Facts were facts.

Office politics is entrenched in work life. For most of us, the word *politics* has something to do with elections, government, and red tape. But the word is defined as the use of power or position to obtain favor within groups of people. Life itself is political, unless you live by yourself on an island.

Another word that suggests what we expect on the job is *meritocracy*: people getting exactly what they earn and deserve, with no nonsense or shenanigans. But of course things never work out that way. When people work together, pecking orders develop, whether official or informal. There are power structures, and some are more skillful at ascertaining and navigating those structures. That gives rise to all kinds of behavior in office settings that can be annoying, deeply unfair, or in some instances, even corrupt.

We all have an instinctive sense of fairness. One of the first complaints children learn is "It's not fair!" And in some particular situations, it may be true. But so is the inevitable reply from Mom or Dad: "Life isn't fair." So when we come to office life, we're no longer fighting over a toy or a later bedtime. We're competing for a promotion or some other life enhancement. Or we're being laid off, even though we've never worked harder or better. The stakes are higher, and the emotions are more amplified.

Which brings us back to employment at will. The court system has no time or resources to sift through every dismissal or missed promotion to ascertain its empirical fairness. These things are ultimately subjective anyway. Life is going to be as unfair in the workplace as anywhere else, and office politics will play into it. Supervisors and managers can be arbitrary, unethical, unjust, and biased, but that doesn't make their actions illegal or actionable.

Many men and women walk into my office with issues that fall under the broad category of office politics. Many, like Ed, say, "They can't do this to me," and the sad fact is that yes, they really can. The law can't and won't begin to navigate the intricacies of interoffice social complexity.

With no real hard and fast rules of engagement, workers will use various tools to gain an advantage. This can manifest itself in a number of ways.

PERSONALITY CONFLICT

What could be more inevitable than people being thrown together in the workplace and finding themselves butting heads? Sooner or later, most of us clash with the boss or a coworker. Sometimes two personalities simply don't gel. But unless this has to do with a worker's inclusion in a protected category—gender, race, or others— the only option is to find a way to get along with the other person.

Perhaps you have a job that's very important to you. You've been in civil service for several years, and you need a few more to qualify for vested benefits. So walking away and finding another job isn't practical or prudent. But you work for a boss who is impossible, and who has taken a dim view of you, for whatever reason. You'll struggle to get decent job reviews, and when assignments are handed out, yours will always be the ones nobody wants.

In such a case, you really have one option: figure out what it takes to improve your relationship with the boss. This may offend your pride. It may seem as if *he's* the one who should be working on improving your relationship. But still, he's the boss, he has all the leverage, and he has broken no laws.

An attorney is not your best option in such a scenario. Nor will the HR department likely help you. These units simply aren't equipped to deal with feelings and personal battles.

A therapist or an industrial psychologist would be far more practical. You need to consult with someone who can help you navigate the treacherous rapids of interpersonal relationships. Your other option, of course, is to do nothing at all and become more and more frustrated and embittered. If this is your boss we're talking about, you can't simply avoid each other. You need to extend an olive branch and find some way to get on better terms. Try setting up a meeting, being honest (though nonconfrontational), and asking what you can do to make the work experience more positive for both of you. This proactive strategy is successful more often than people think.

Perhaps transferring to a different department (again, in the example of civil service) would solve the problem. But when it comes to personal relationships and getting along, we're all on our own in the workplace.

FAVORITISM

A common scenario is when a manager wishes to build his or her own team. It's a difficult situation. The new boss (like JT) knows someone with whom he works effectively, and the company allows him to make the call. It also happens in the case of a merger, when departments from the two companies are mingled, and the larger, more powerful one has the leverage.

The corresponding employee from the other company is out in the cold.

I see these situations in many places, and so do most of us. A new baseball or football coach is hired, and very seldom does he keep the assistant coaches he inherited. He has his own system and friends in coaching who have helped him for years. Even in churches, synagogues, and places of worship, new clergy will come in and bring their own people. But the new people displace some of the old.

If it's as simple as that, again, no law is being broken, assuming those replaced are not in the protected categories. I tend to advise those getting new bosses that it's a good time to look around, to update the resume, and to be prepared to make a move if necessary. This doesn't mean taking flight whenever there's a management change; it's simply the recognition that no job is forever, and there are times when the only option is to find another position.

PROCESS CHANGES

The next category also involves a new boss. But this time the changes aren't in personnel but procedures.

That may be the very reason a new manager is brought in—the need for shaking things up and doing things differently. The new boss has been a big success somewhere else. She turned around a struggling department at the EFG Corporation, and she promises to come in and do the same thing in your company. The good news is that she isn't importing a team; the bad news is that she's importing all kinds of ideas and strategies that aren't the way you've always done things. Those who come to me in distress tend to be convinced there was nothing wrong with the old way. We tend to be creatures of habit, and change is disconcerting. Perhaps these employees have just a few years until retirement. Why should they have to change now?

As long as she's not asking you to do anything illegal, bypass OSHA regulations, or circumvent the rules in some other way, she has the go-ahead to insist on these new ways.

Perhaps you, as the employee, are right, and the old ways are the best ways. It's really immaterial because there's no legal recourse for this situation. You have to adapt to a new situation, as uncomfortable as that may be, or ask for a transfer to a new department, or start looking for a new position in another company.

I've mentioned protected categories. If there are issues of gender, race, disability, or age involved, for example, you might have some leverage in negotiation. In that case, given that you clearly won't hang on to the job, you could possibly negotiate a severance package. The company wants a swift and clean transition, and for you to sign a release. That way a lawsuit could be avoided down the road. At times our clients have managed to come away with a reasonable settlement in those conditions.

In the case of Ed, however, none of those issues applied. Ed was experienced but not nearing retirement, he had no physical disabilities, and he was the same race and gender as his replacement. He realized it was time to decide between accepting a transfer or looking for new employment.

ACCEPT THE NEW REALITY

Issues of office politics—particularly when our little corner of the workplace is challenged—become very personal. It becomes us versus them, who will win, and who will lose. Yet most of that is entirely psychological. If we have to leave a company, or if someone gets a promotion that we felt we deserved, it may feel like losing, but that's a matter of pride. Who's to say we've lost anything? The promotion we didn't get may turn out to be a bad job. The effect of being forced out of a company may turn out to be a bright new beginning, better than anything we could have hoped. We've all seen that happen in life through many kinds of circumstances. I'm not sure how many times I've heard people say, "Getting fired was the best thing that ever happened to me." It's a lot.

A lost job or a lost marriage quite often ends up liberating someone to do something new and exciting. So the beginning of handling these situations is to view them as objectively as possible, and that means avoiding thoughts of winners and losers. This is a decision point, a crossroad, and we simply have to get all the information and figure out our best strategy rather than emotionally focusing on who is at fault.

I also find myself counseling people on a personal level more than a legal level when it comes to office politics. Some people become deeply anxious and stressed because of the way things operate in the workplace. The wrong people do get those promotions at times. Some people are very skillful at avoiding the real work and manipulating the more compliant into taking it on. The meek shall inherit the workload.

There are poor team members, gossips, backstabbers, and those who flatter and fawn over those in management positions. Nobody enjoys watching these hijinks. But my advice is that we should steer well clear of politics, rather than getting sucked into it, and work to make ourselves indispensable. It's the one true defense against being mistreated—knowing the job and doing it as well as it can be done. Excellence is a powerful shield.

There are a number of good books, from Dale Carnegie to Stephen Covey and beyond, that are helpful in making us the most valuable assets in our workplaces. I find that people tend to stop reading those books once they get beyond their twenties, but the most successful people are the ones who keep reading, keep stretching, keep trying to find some new angle or some way to have a slight edge over those around them. Flattering the boss is superficial, and you can bet the boss sees through it. But serving the boss by getting the work done and going beyond the expected will get us noticed. Employment at will means you can easily be fired. Becoming indispensable removes the boss's temptation.

I've had clients who engaged executive coaches to help them be more successful in the workplace. Others have worked with therapists. I've even seen people go to marriage counselors to help them understand how to save their relationship with the boss. No, they didn't take the boss with them to their appointments, but they treated their job as a relationship commitment and approached counseling with the idea of considering personal changes to make things work.

Most important of all is to accept the new reality. It's not often that a company will change course for individual employees and their grievances. No matter how unfair we think the system may be, businesses will do what they think is best for the bottom line, and we can either adapt or move on. My observation is that there's an innate skill to functioning in a social situation. For the socially adept, it comes easily enough, and they thrive without even having to think about it. Their instincts work toward making the most of relationships with the people around them, including supervisors.

Others, perhaps more introverted, lack that skill. Work situations will be difficult for them almost regardless of the particular company. Difficult relationships are traumatic. But I tell these latter types, "Don't worry about that. You don't have to try becoming something you're not. Just study the tactics of thriving in the workplace. You may not have been born with the talent, but you can learn the fundamentals."

I've also suggested that inertia can be our enemy. That is, we shouldn't begin to think any current position is the only one we should ever have and that our only future is to stay where we are. We never know what lies beyond that next door. I've known many people who fought a war to hang on to the misery of their current employment, only to find that the next position was exponentially better, happier, and healthier for them. But again, many of us aren't particularly adventurous. We look at it as "the devil we know" versus "the devil we won't know" when the next place may not bedevil us at all.

My advice: if you're not happy where you are, think about the reasons for it. How much of it is due to a bad workplace? There are many of those. How much of it is due to you? That's the harder question, isn't it? The right mindset tends to make the toughest jobs more pleasant, and the wrong mindset can make the best job wretched. That's something to think about, though this is a question for therapy or religion rather than an attorney.

Know thyself, as the Greeks have counseled us, and think about the future. Where would you look for new work if the need arose? Every employee should spend time reflecting on that question. It could become relevant at any time.

This chapter has been geared for the workforce, but it's a topic for business leaders as well. Office politics may be unavoidable, but it's a drain on productivity that needs to be limited. For many reasons, these situations won't be reported to the top executives. But for example, if there's a division chief who has high turnover, the culture in that department should be examined closely. People should be interviewed and encouraged to talk without fear of reprisal. It may be that an outside consultant can come in, do a study, and offer suggestions that could make for a healthier work environment. It's a good subject for a little proactive movement by CEOs and executives because a strong, fair, and fully cooperative workplace will lead to higher profits, happier people, and far fewer lawsuits.

CHAPTER 7

DISCRIMINATION

J ADA WAS AN ART INSTRUCTOR AT A MIDWESTERN university—and like many instructors of art, she was a talented artist in her own right. Her field of expertise was African American and urban art. While she was the only person of color on the art faculty, she was deeply respected by her peers and quite popular with students.

It happened that the dean of the art school was retiring, and Jada was sorry to see him go. He was her mentor in the academic world and a good friend. He had helped her since she'd become an instructor at the college level, and he'd also promoted her as an artist.

When his replacement was introduced at a faculty reception, Jada noticed something odd. Dean Lawrence, the new addition, shook the hands of each current faculty member as they came through the reception line—except for that of Jada. She didn't like to be overly sensitive, and perhaps it could be dismissed as an oversight. But the moment, and the dean's abrupt stiffness, was awkward enough to make her wonder.

Her suspicions increased as Dean Lawrence presided at his first faculty meetings. He would call on various professors and assistants, but never Jada. As he wouldn't make eye contact, Jada felt invisible. She forced the issue by speaking up and addressing him directly, and again, he was rather cool to her.

Then one day she walked into the building lobby and was shocked to see that the display featuring her art had been removed. Jada asked a few questions and discovered that her paintings had been moved to a closet, and yes, this had been done at the request of Dean Lawrence. The removal certainly transformed the area, for the striking African motifs had given way to American heartland art that apparently the new dean favored.

Jada made a mental note. She found herself doing that more and more.

Then, on two occasions, Dean Lawrence referred to Jada as a "knucklehead." She never heard him utter a derogatory term to describe any other member of the faculty, nor was the dean's tone of voice the same in other instances of talking about professors and instructors. He spoke to her and about her as if she were an annoyance, a nuisance.

When the new term began, Jada noticed her course load had decreased. One of her classes had been cut from the curriculum. By now, she knew what to expect and began to anticipate the possible loss of her position. Sure enough, her contract wasn't renewed at the end of the year. A white male instructor was soon hired in her place.

Jada filed a suit based on racial discrimination, and to make a long story shorter—she was successful.

Racial discrimination can be difficult to prove. The dean was never going to directly refer to Jada's racial characteristics. Nor was he foolish enough to make general comments that would identify him as a racist. Of course, for each and every one of his questionable actions in the case of Jada, he had a ready excuse. For example, "knucklehead" was a joking and affectionate label, he insisted. The lobby? It was due for a fresh look, and he simply sought a theme that would contrast with the previous one. And as he told it, he cut Jada's course load based on legitimate opinions about what the students needed.

But as we've observed, juries are sharp and observant. Once they're seated, in my experience, they take their assignment seriously. They listen to evidence and make reasonable judgments based on sworn testimony. In this case, there were simply too many indications of the dean's viewpoint. His explanations simply didn't wash. Jada had been a victim of racial discrimination, and the ruling went in her favor.

Sadly enough, race is still an issue in our world. Perhaps it always will be. Of course, there are other kinds of discrimination as well—gender, age, nationality, religion, and disability are all categories protected by federal law. What do companies need to know to avoid even the appearance of discrimination, which can be as problematic as the real thing? What do employees need to know about what constitutes it and what does not?

THE PROBLEM OF BIAS

The United States is both a melting pot of many nationalities, creeds, and colors and a nation uniquely committed to equality and freedom for all. As a result, discrimination is an issue that is always current. To discriminate is to draw active distinctions between various categories, such as those I've listed. The Civil Rights Act of 1964 is the centerpiece of federal policy on this issue. This came about after years of new laws and amendments, beginning with the Civil Rights Act of 1866 and gradually taking an ever-tighter stance against various forms of unjust bias—in schools, in voting, and in public life. The 1964 act, in particular, was transformational legislation for the workplace.

DISCRIMINATION

Title VII of the act protects employees and job applicants from employment discrimination based on race, color, religion, sex, and national origin. Every employment issue, from recruitment, hiring, firing, and other decisions about employment, is covered by Title VII. The Civil Rights Act of 1991 fine-tuned the 1964 act and strengthened the protections of previous ones.

The law is clear. Women can't be turned down for jobs simply on the basis of their gender. Employees can't be fired on the basis of advanced age. And restaurants can't refuse to hire or serve people of color as they did in some regions prior to the Civil Rights era.

Even more than half a century after this momentous congressional act, the question of bias remains a heated one in American life and thought. People can't legally discriminate, but they still carry personal biases, which are generally socially unacceptable. As a result, we use language carefully to avoid the appearance of sexism, racism, or some other bias, knowing we mean well. There's an inherent tension to these topics.

As a result, those who do harbor bias tend to use selective wording, allowing them plausible denial in any accusation of bias. We talk about the "dog whistle," which is a way of conveying a message without stating it explicitly. Even the dean from our case study avoided racist terminology; his problem was more in the accumulation of actions and visible attitudes.

No single piece of evidence would have been enough—certainly not the lack of shaking someone's hand. The combination of elements, however, made a strong case. And the closest thing to a "smoking gun" may have come when Jada had her class load changed and no other instructors did. That's discrimination in a nutshell: different treatment than others on the basis of skin color or some other status.

This is why those who would make a case for being victims of discrimination must have strong and thorough records. Discrimination is rarely indiscrete. It prefers to lurk just out of plain view.

PROTECTED CLASSES

Illegal discrimination on the job is the antithesis of employment at will, a policy that allows a great deal of freedom in hiring and firing. It's the exception to the rule. No one can be dismissed on account of race, gender, or other facts, but the burden is still on the employee to demonstrate that this was truly the basis of the firing. In a previous chapter, I described the case of the custodian who told me he'd been fired because he was "an old Black man." He was naming two protected classes: age and race. But he couldn't demonstrate either of these as being the basis for his firing, and in fact, his chronic tardiness was the reason for the dismissal, even if a

DISCRIMINATION

better solution would have been closer and more compassionate communication.

A protected class isn't absolutely protected. There still needs to be evidence that Title VII has been violated. If you make a case for discrimination, the first question is whether you belong to a protected category. Then you must show that you suffered an adverse employment action, whether it was losing out on a job opportunity, being fired, being demoted, or some term or condition of your employment. Finally, you must demonstrate that someone outside your category got that job or received better treatment.

Then you must deal with the defendant's line of reasoning. Why were you treated differently, or were you not treated differently at all? Why was this or was this not an adverse employment action? And so forth. In our case study, the university claimed Jada's contract was not renewed because the department had decided not to offer those courses. It's true that the courses weren't immediately reoffered, but in the following semester, they were—so this argument didn't hold up in the eyes of the jury.

Still, the most difficult point is proving the intention to discriminate. It's not enough to be treated unfairly as part of a protected category. Proving intent is always the most difficult hurdle in certain kinds of cases, including discrimination. Racism, sexism, ageism, and other forms of bias are essentially attitudes. How can mental attitudes be empirically proven? It simply requires enough plain evidence to show a credible pattern. In the case of the dean at the university, there weren't one or two pieces of evidence but an impressive body of evidential factors.

In trying to demonstrate prejudice, we have to deal with the aforementioned "dog whistles." Let's say the dean made certain statements that conveyed a meaning without using, in this case, racial terminology. We would bring in industrial psychologists or sociologists to help identify common dog whistles and behaviors and place them in social context. What the dean said, taken by itself, may seem innocuous. But if the jury understands the history of those words being used in such contexts, bias could be demonstrated more convincingly.

Then you must tell a story, using all these elements in social context. Here is a woman teaching art from African and urban cultures. She's popular with the students, and her own art is on display. The big change in all of that comes when a new dean enters the picture, refuses to shake her hand, treats her poorly in front of her peers in public, removes her art from the lobby, decreases her course load, then chooses not to renew her contract. There are also elements of a Black woman gaining a position of authority, then being pushed back. Then, the epilogue to the story is the way white instructors were treated entirely differently. The other members of the faculty can be listed, and it could be shown that none of them had courses cut or contracts lost. This part is often more difficult because some of the other faculty members might not have been as sensitive to some of these cues.

It could be that the dean's failure to shake Jada's hand was inadvertent. Why he failed is the question. Was it because he intentionally avoided a black person? Or Was it because he was distracted? What is important is if there is a pattern of discrimination. Was the dean's prejudice expressed often, not just once or twice. Without direct evidence of discriminatory intent you must prove such intent with circumstantial evidence.

Still, all the elements are there for an attorney to paint that picture for the jury and demonstrate that this is a classic case of discrimination—especially since the jury brings its own life experience and observations to the courtroom.

Let's examine the categories protected from discrimination. As you'll see, the basic practice of discrimination within these categories is clear federal law, but lawmakers have also been careful to cut off as many "loopholes" as possible. For example, employers can't schedule interviews on particular holy days of a certain religion in order to create a situation excluding people of a certain faith from applying for a job. And in many cases, employers must make allowances for those from protected categories, such as assignments given to someone pregnant or reasonable cooperation with the requirements of religious practice.

NATIONAL ORIGIN

After the attacks on September 11, 2001, discrimination on the basis of national origin became a particularly relevant issue in the United States. Even in an age of terror, there could be no discrimination simply because of one's country of origin.

- It's unlawful to discriminate against an employee or potential employee on the basis of national origin. This includes discrimination because the employee comes from a particular place, because she is a member of an ethnic group, because she has an accent, or because it is believed that the employee has some particular ethnic background.

- This ban applies to hiring and firing as well as promotion, pay, job training, or any other term, condition, or privilege of employment.

- Association with persons of some national origin is also protected, whether through marriage, friendship, ethnic organizations, or some groups, or traditionally ethnic churches and schools.

DISCRIMINATION

- Employers may not discriminate on the basis of a condition that predominantly affects a given ethnicity, unless it can be proven that the presence of the condition somehow affects the business adversely.

- Harassment of employees due to their national origin is forbidden, whether by the employer, coworkers, or third persons at the worksite.

- Businesses may not segregate employees on the basis of national origin.

- Accent discrimination is impermissible under most circumstances. Similarly, English fluency rules are permissible only if it can be demonstrated that they are required for the effective performance of the position for which they are imposed.

- English-only rules are acceptable only if they are adopted for nondiscriminatory reasons, such as workplace safety.

PREGNANCY

- Pregnancy, childbirth, and related medical conditions are protected categories.

- The marital status of pregnant women is also protected from discrimination. Pregnancy-related benefits must be extended to married and single workers alike.

- Employers may not refuse to hire a pregnant woman unless the pregnancy would prevent her from performing major functions of her job.

- If the employee becomes temporarily unable to perform her job due to pregnancy-related conditions, the employer must treat her the same as any temporarily disabled employee. For example, the employer may provide modified tasks, alternative assignments, disability leave, or leave without pay.

- The employer may not require the employee to remain on leave until the birth of the child if she recovers from the pregnancy-related condition and is able to work.

- Pregnant employees must be permitted to work as long as they are able to perform their job.

RACE AND COLOR

- Employees and potential employees are protected from discrimination on the basis of race or color.

DISCRIMINATION

- This applies to hiring and firing as well as promotion, pay, job training, or any other term, condition or privilege of employment.

- Association with persons of some race or color is also protected, including marriage, friendship, ethnic organizations of groups, or traditionally ethnic churches and schools.

- While racial characteristics are varied, discrimination against any individual on the basis of unalterable characteristics is prohibited.

- Employers may not discriminate on the basis of a condition that predominantly affects a given race, unless it can be proven that the presence of the condition somehow affects the business adversely.

- Harassment of employees due to their race or color, whether by the employer, coworkers, or third persons at the worksite, is forbidden under federal laws.

- Employees can't be segregated on the basis of race or color.

RELIGION

This is another category that became more relevant in the wake of the terrorist attack in 2001.

- It is unlawful to discriminate against an employee or potential employee on the basis of religion. No particular faith or the following of a particular creed should open an employee or potential employee to discrimination.

- This ban applies to hiring and firing, promotion, pay, job training, and any other term, condition, or privilege of employment.

- Association with persons of a particular religion is also protected, whether through marriage, friendship, ethnic organizations, or groups, or churches and schools.

- Employers must also provide reasonable accommodation for the religious practices of their employees, unless doing so would create undue hardship on the employer.

- The scheduling of job selection activities that are in conflict with an employee's religious needs is prohibited by the law.

DISCRIMINATION

- Furthermore, restrictive dress codes and the refusal to allow observance of the Sabbath or religious holidays is a violation of the law, unless it can be proven that not doing so would cause undue hardship.

- Harassment of employees due to their religion, whether by the employer or by coworkers, is forbidden under federal laws.

- An employee whose religious beliefs prohibit the payment of union dues cannot be required to pay the dues but may pay an equivalent amount to a charitable organization.

SEX

Sex discrimination is discrimination of any type based on a person's sex or sexual identity.

AGE

These cases have become more common as a huge sector of the American population—the baby boomers—have reached retirement age without desiring retirement.

Can a sixty-eight-year-old man claim age discrimination because computer skills were required? Probably not, because the company would, in all probability, be able to demonstrate the importance of those computer skills. If the aging worker couldn't handle the changes, his dismissal wouldn't violate the law. However, a company has no right to assume those over a certain age "can't keep up." The employees must receive every opportunity to do the work.

All fifty states have passed laws forbidding discrimination on the basis of age, and the Age Discrimination in Employment Act of 1967 established federal law to restrict people from being penalized in the workplace simply on the basis of advanced age. In some states, younger workers are protected from "reverse age discrimination."

It's unlawful to establish a mandatory retirement age, with certain sensible exceptions. In one notable case, an airline was allowed to require its pilots to retire at the age of sixty. There have been many cases in which employees were fired just before qualifying for pensions or other benefits. Plaintiffs must prove that the timing of the firing was not coincidental and that some other factor wasn't the real reason for the dismissal.

DISABILITIES

The Americans with Disabilities Act of 1990 added those with disabilities as a protected category. This law forbids discrimination against a qualified person with a disability. Companies cannot use a disability as a reason to refuse to hire or promote a worker, to terminate a worker, or to deny a worker privileges and conditions of employment. Reasonable accommodations are required of companies, such as making facilities accessible and job restructuring.

The ADA protects a person who has a record of having a disability or who is regarded as having a disability. The ADA also contains special rules about how employers can question employees about their physical or mental condition, including the administration of physical or psychological tests.

Current users of illegal drugs are not protected by the ADA, and employers may test their employees for current drug use. Former drug use, however, may be protected.

REMEDIES AND DAMAGES

Those who prevail legally against businesses in discrimination cases might expect certain remedies. In other words, there are strict and prescribed limits on how much money a court can award you if you "win" and for only certain kinds of harms. Lawyers call these the "elements of damages."

Every case has two equally important parts: liability and damages. Liability is whether or not the company broke the law. In other words, did the company fire you because you are a member of a protected class or engaged in protected activity? If so, they are liable for the damages they caused for which the law will allow you to recover.

To put it in more universal terms. If a driver runs a red light he is liable for any damages he might cause. The act itself does not dictate the amount of civil damages he is responsible to pay.

Damages are the monetary amount a driver must pay if he actually hits a pedestrian or another vehicle. Depending on the victim's injuries, hospital bills, pain and suffering, and loss of income (off work due to the crash) the amount of damages can go up or down.

Many insurance companies and juries will measure pain and suffering by the amount of medical bills. They assume that if someone has $20,000.00 in medical bills that person's pain and suffering is 10x the suffering of someone with $2,000.00 in medical bills. The proof might prove otherwise—but that is a rule of thumb.

ELEMENTS OF DAMAGES FOR EMPLOYMENT CASES

The elements of damages in an employment case are:

- Back pay
- Reinstatement or Front Pay
- Compensatory
- Punitive
- Attorneys' Fees and Costs

DISCRIMINATION

Back pay is the difference between the dollar amount of your compensation (money and benefits) your company paid to you before the illegal adverse employment action (demotion, suspension, termination, failure to promote or hire) and what compensation and benefits you actually receive before you settle your case or you receive a jury verdict.

Frankly, back pay is a very important element of damage and really drives the value of a discrimination case. Most of a settlement is going to be based on back pay and how long it will take to make the plaintiff whole.

The employer is usually required to pay the full value of lost wages. But the plaintiff bears a duty to mitigate those damages by making reasonable efforts to find comparable employment after the job termination. This is why it can be very difficult to settle such cases quickly, particularly with highly compensated persons. If an executive is reemployed after just a few weeks or months the back pay will be much lower than if they can never work again and are five to ten years to retirement.

Often people can find a job that pays 20 percent to 40 percent or more, less than their previous job. This will provide ongoing back pay damages.

Reinstatement. The law favors reinstatement as the default remedy for future employment. The drafters of Title VII in particular wanted to create an integrated workforce not merely allow employers to maintain an all white all mate workforce by simply "paying victims off." As the years progressed and more companies integrated and grew more diversity and it became apparent that reinstating someone who filed a complaint against a company was not healthy for either side the courts allowed more and more settlements and judgments to include another remedy.

Front Pay. Sometimes, when reinstatement of the employee isn't realistic, or if the employee refuses reinstatement, front pay can be assigned. It compensates the employee for future losses. Front pay is an extension of the calculation of back pay, just forward from the date of settlement or verdict.

Front pay is an equitable remedy, meaning that it arises out of the Court's power to do equity. Such equitable remedies are unique to each case and usually up to the judge, not the jury. Plaintiffs usually need an expert witness, an economist or vocational rehabilitation expert, or both, the experts set the plaintiff's expected future earnings based on their age, occupation, industry, locale, and other factors.

Compensatory damages may be awarded for emotional stress, pain and suffering, inconvenience, mental anguish, and loss of enjoyment of life.

Punitive damages are awarded in those cases in which the discrimination is judged intentional and with malice or reckless indifference to the individual's rights. These are less common. They are meant to punish the wrongdoer to deter future illegal conduct.

The federal law and most state laws cap the amount of compensatory and punitive damages you can recover. It depends on the size of the employer, but the MOST you can recover for compensatory and punitive damages combined is $300,000.00 under federal law and most state laws.

Atttorney's fees, court costs, and **expenses.** Title VII and most employment discrimination statutes allow for the worker to recover her atttorney's fees, court costs, and expenses, if she wins. The amount of these fees are either negotiated in the case of a settlement or the worker files a petition with the court after a successful trial and the court may award all or some of her fees and expenses incurred.

Discrimination can be difficult to prove, particularly if it is carried out shrewdly. For there to be a viable case, documentation and multiple pieces of evidence are required. But this is one of the primary protections we have for fairness in the workplace. Nobody should become the subject of discrimination in the universal need to earn a living.

CHAPTER 8

HOSTILE WORK ENVIRONMENT

Activist Tarana Burke is credited with being the first to use the phrase "Me too," on social media in relation to sexual assault. That was back in 2006, and the forum was MySpace, the now-forgotten website. It wasn't until October 2017 that the case of movie producer Harvey Weinstein caused the Me Too movement to become a national phenomenon. Actress Alyssa Milano encouraged the use of #MeToo as a Twitter hashtag to showcase the universality of problems with sexual harassment and assault and to demonstrate just how many people have been the victims of sexual harassment.

The idea was to motivate women who'd been reluctant to come forward in the past. Since there is strength in numbers, this would be the moment for them to show courage and admit to some experience of sexual assault or harassment.

As the movement went viral, there was tremendous fallout, particularly in the world of celebrities and even in politics. Many women testified to treatment ranging from inappropriate to violent. A national dialogue ensued on how sexuality is handled and mishandled in the workplace.

Federal law tells us that when someone's workplace behavior creates an environment that is sufficiently difficult or uncomfortable for someone else, due to discrimination, a hostile work environment is defined. Sexual harassment, suggestive remarks, unwanted touching, the showing of suggestive photographs, and sexual language and jokes are the most common expressions of these complaints, though nationality, race, and other factors can also become part of the problem.

There's always the problem of where to draw the line. Men (as the gender most often implicated) will insist they were just telling a joke, teasing, or simply showing innocent affection and that it was all a matter of misunderstanding. And to some extent, that could be true because for many years, such things were deemed acceptable, and women rarely complained. For one thing, there could be retaliation if a problem was caused. For another, they were likely to be ignored and branded as troublemakers. And in a workplace largely controlled by men, they might have felt a great deal of insecurity about their job stability.

The unspoken message was that "boys will be boys," and it's best to be a good sport and try to fit in. So it's at least conceivable that in this kind of culture, some men misjudged the boundaries. But clearly, the boundaries should have been there all along, and the aggressors should have known better.

There are other nonsexual forms of workplace hostility. Race, national origin, age, religion, disability are protected categories upon which a company cannot base a hostile working environment.

Companies cannot creat a hostile working environment because you engaged protected activity such as: taking Family Medical Leave, complaining about illegal working conditions or compensation schemes (minimum wage violations or overtime violations)

For example, in a certain state state troopers attempted to make a young officer miserable enough to resign after he refused to falsify an arrest record. He was then subjected to various forms of harassment. Sometimes heightened discipline, reduced hours or pay rates, or unwanted transfers to another location have qualified as this type of treatment, and of course, those actions qualify as evidence if a complaint is filed.

Being a bad boss alone doesn't qualify as harassment. Otherwise, we'd lose a massive number of managers from our workforce. According to one survey, two of every three resigning workers have blamed a bad boss. Nor are ordinary teasing, joking, or on-the-job disputes covered. There are unpleasant social factors connected to every form of employment.

The true measure of a hostile work environment is that when doing your job becomes impossible due to someone's actions, communication, or behavior. The reasonable expectations of a comfortable work environment must have been altered in a discriminatory manner. That means, as we've seen in our chapter on that topic, that the company's conduct is motivated by a person's sex, race, national origin, age, etc... If the company or a boss is "mean" to everyone, then the conduct may not be illegal. What follows is an example from our practice of hostile workplace conditions.

"BRO CULTURE"

We represented Jane, a woman who was a trader for a commodities firm. She was highly professional and one of the firm's more accomplished traders. Yet she was treated by others as if she were a support person. Like other women, Jane disliked these conditions but knew there was little she could do about it. If she wanted to work in this industry, she had to

HOSTILE WORK ENVIRONMENT

take it as it was, she was told—at least, up to a point. And she had a good idea of what that breaking point might be.

The firm prioritized the comfort of the male producers. The dignity of female employees wasn't much of a consideration. This was a boys' club with almost a frat-house feel, with a lot of testosterone-fueled joking and competition. This phenomenon, observed in new business startups and male-dominant industries, has been called "bro culture."

That was the case at this firm, and the men felt that nothing was out of bounds, whether it was verbally demeaning the women, touching them inappropriately, and making off-color remarks just to get a reaction.

Though this was commodities trading, the men seemed to identify themselves with the "Masters of the Universe" idea from Tom Wolfe's novel *Bonfire of the Vanities*. "We're the stock traders, we create capital, and therefore we can behave exactly the way we want."

Underlining the difference between the genders was the pay disparity. Jane pulled her weight but brought home less money than a male trader would have for the same work. She came mostly on the basis of the pay equity issue, but it was clear that this was only one part of a hostile work environment.

During the depositions and during the trial itself, we talked to various women who came forward to discuss how they were treated in this firm. One of these was a trade assistant. Her job was to move back and forth between the trading floor and various offices, delivering documents and messages in both directions. The trading floor was arranged a bit like a reverse amphitheater. You walked in at the top, through double doors, and the desks circled the center. The "stage" area was actually the trading desk in the center.

The trade assistant told us that she would stand on the other side of those doors, getting ready to walk down and past those desks, and put on her "mental armor." It would take her fifteen to twenty seconds to prepare herself for everything she was about to encounter. Then she'd take a deep breath and "run the gauntlet," walking through those rows of desks and blocking out everything so she could focus on getting her job done. There would be all kinds of comments about her physical appearance, inappropriate suggestions, some of them specific, touches in places where she didn't want to be touched, and being hugged when she didn't want to be hugged. Every man in the room, she said, felt entitled and encouraged to objectify her, though she clearly didn't encourage anything like that. She would complete her errand, escape, take off the "armor," and then wait for the next assignment, when she'd have to do it all again.

Hers was the most eloquent testimony, but she wasn't the only one who told that story. It was a hostile work environment for women, and the firm seemed to care about nothing other than enabling the men to have their fun. It was an easy case to prove because the culture of degradation was so consistent and so all-encompassing. This wasn't just one woman's personal experience but a problem for everyone.

If you're a business leader whose company has that kind of culture, with a permanent environment of hostility for employees, you have to deal with that and eliminate it, first, because it's the right thing to do, and second, because your business is opening itself to extreme financial and legal liability as well as terribly adverse publicity.

As we've discussed elsewhere, company culture is all-important. When the culture becomes this dysfunctional, a great deal of work needs to be done to make corrections. New rules and employee training are probably warranted.

If you're the one being harassed in some way, speak up, and get good legal advice. It's not just your business but a problem for others who might be harassed. Think about the number of women who failed to speak up in the commodities firm. It seems incredible that conditions could continue along those lines for any length of time. But they did, until Jane stepped forward with her story.

I'm told that the firm made some fairly dramatic changes after it was finally forced to own up to its problem. Strict rules were put into place concerning how women could be treated. More women were hired, and they were paid in accordance with how men were paid. This wasn't a matter of doing what was politically acceptable; it was good business. The firm found a great many talented female traders and also cleaned out some of the men who had not only contributed to the problem but weren't particularly productive. That was a lesson in itself. It stands to reason that those who would treat women so poorly have other problems. They may be trying to fit in or attract attention to themselves. They might well have self-esteem or power issues. When the firm upgraded its ethics and behavior, it found that its profitability jumped as well.

HOW DO YOU MEASURE "HOSTILE"?

The tough question is deciding whether a hostile work environment is an illegally hostile work environment. Some workplaces can be very difficult and troubling without crossing that line into violation of federal law. One study suggests that one in five workers experiences a hostile work environment of some type.[4] A boss may seem to bully a certain employee or a group of them. A coworker may give someone a hard time. It makes a difference whether someone is

---

4   Maestas et al., *Working Conditions in the United States: Results of the 2015 American Working Conditions Survey* (Santa Monica: RAND Corporation, 2017).

HOSTILE WORK ENVIRONMENT

a member of a protected category and whether that category figures into the harassment. Then it becomes a case of discrimination.

The US Supreme Court stated in one of its decisions, *Oncale v. Sundowner Offshore Services, Inc.*, that the Civil Rights Act of 1964, Title VII, is "not a general civility code."[5] The courts cannot determine the extent of good manners in the workplace. Thus teasing or behavior that isn't particularly serious is discounted. The key for serious charges is whether the treatment has negatively affected the work conditions of the employees and whether that can be demonstrated.

The US Equal Employment Opportunity Commission (EEOC) sets legal criteria for determining whether a hostile work environment may be violating federal law. There are three qualifications. First, the harassment is based on one of the protected categories described in the previous chapter. Second, it must be more than a single incident; it must be part of a long-lasting pattern. And third, the degree of severity must be enough that the workplace environment becomes intolerable (intimidating, offensive, or abusive).

The third category, of course, allows for subjectivity. This is why a plaintiff would need to demonstrate an objective

---

5   Oncale v. Sundowner Offshore Services, Inc., 523 U.S. 75 (1998), https://supreme.justia.com/cases/federal/us/523/75/.

change in work conditions and performance. It must be clear that it's become impossible for the worker to continue doing his or her job effectively.

What about management? Has a manager witnessed the behavior or been made aware of it? The treatment should always be reported. If it's on record, the employer now bears responsibility for addressing the issue and will be liable if nothing changes.

Once a claim is filed, EEOC regulators will be called upon to investigate the accusations and see if they meet the standard criteria. The victim will bear the burden of proof to make his or her case. Regulators will examine all evidence, including the nature and context of the conduct. Judgment of whether the harassment is severe or pervasive enough to be illegal is made on a case-by-case basis.

Behavior that falls short of the standard criteria may not be illegal, but it can still be intolerable and unnecessary. An environment for work should be just that, and social conditions should never be allowed to make it uncomfortable. A good manager won't allow it and will have procedures in place to address the behavior. Again, establishing rules is the right thing to do, and it's also good business. Difficult personal situations definitely hamper production. They increase turnover, which cuts into profit. So there's no reason to allow the conditions of a hostile work environment.

If for some reason nothing is done—and that can happen, since many businesses are very poorly operated—then your only options are to fight for better treatment within the company by hiring a lawyer, filing an EEOC complaint, and bringing a lawsuit if necessary or to find a better place of employment. Acceptance of offensive treatment is never a solution.

CHAPTER 9

WHISTLE BLOWING

JAMES BOBRESKI WAS A PROCESS CONTROL TECHNIcian in 1999. He was a contract worker whose company was serving a wastewater treatment plant in Washington, DC. It's the largest plant of its kind in the world. Bobreski's job was to review all the routine processes and make sure they were running efficiently as wastewater from homes and other facilities, coming through sewers and pumping stations, was collected and treated. This is a crucially important procedure that controls and neutralizes pollution and hazardous sewage.

Bobreski didn't like what he was seeing. The chlorine gas alarms weren't functioning, and there had been a massive chlorine gas leak. Hundreds of tons of liquid chlorine was being stored improperly and illegally. It's important to understand that chlorine in this form is toxic and poisonous. Bobreski discovered that the leaks had become so regular that workers were disconnecting the alarms rather than actually dealing with the problem they signaled. If even a small amount of the chlorine had been accidentally released in this form, plant workers would have been killed in seconds, and a poisonous plume more than thirty miles long could have been released. The plant was in a heavily populated area.

Bobreski reported the problems he found and waited for the necessary repairs to begin, but nothing happened. He wasn't one to shrug his shoulders and move on. When the engineer persisted in filing reports and warning about the dangers of the situation, he was told to keep his mouth shut. The Water and Sewer Authority told Bobreski's engineering firm that he had to be fired, or the firm would lose its million-dollar contract with the facility. So eventually he was laid off, but not before he had tape-recorded comments from his supervisor warning him that Bobreski was going to lose the company its lucrative contract if he didn't start looking the other way. These comments ended up in the *Washington*

Post, whom Bobreski contacted with his full story. Two OSHA investigations of the facility were launched.

Bobreski retained attorneys who specialized in whistleblower cases and filed a lawsuit. The plant had few options for defending itself. Spokesmen branded Bobreski as a troublemaker who was exaggerating the dangers of the leaks and the malfunctioning alarms.

The Department of Labor, however, saw the situation quite differently, and the engineer and his cause prevailed. Bobreski had been unfairly dismissed after simply notifying his supervisors about a serious problem. The Department of Labor ordered the Water and Sewer Authority to pay the plaintiff $56,000 in fines, punitive damages, and legal fees—and, most importantly to Bobreski, the plant was ordered to remove the dangerous chlorine and ensure that the alarms were working and heeded.

All Bobreski's actions, including speaking to the press, were justified under whistleblower protection laws. He had triggered two important inspections. If not, who knows what type of environmental disaster could have transpired?

PROTECTION FOR TRUTH TELLERS

Everyone recognizes the importance of whistleblowing to our businesses and political institutions. The greatest danger, of course, is the fear of retaliation. We're told, "If you see something, say something." But the wrath of an employer is no small concern. What if we're fired? What if we're privately threatened? What if nobody wants to hire us because we "snitched"?

A series of federal laws protects whistleblowers so they can feel free to come forward with critical information without fear of the consequences. As we'll see, of course, those consequences still deserve serious consideration.

The 1989 Whistleblower Protection Act (WPA) is the centerpiece of these protections. It enables citizens to report "violation of any law, rule, or regulation, or mismanagement… gross waste of funds, an abuse of authority, or a substantial and specific danger to public health and safety."[6]

Executive Order 12731, which was issued a year later, actually requires all federal employees to "disclose waste, fraud, abuse, and corruption" to those in authority. The idea is that reporting serious, dangerous, or unethical problems isn't just an option—it's a responsibility and therefore a legal requirement.

Then in 2012, the Whistleblower Protection Enhancement Act (WPEA) filled in some of the gaps to protect truth tellers by expanding the penalties for those who violated the WPA protections by coming after those who spoke out. Five years

---

6   "Prohibited Personnel Practice 8: Whistleblower Protection," U.S. Merit Systems Protection Board, accessed November 4, 2022, https://www.mspb.gov/ppp/8ppp.htm.

later, a new Whistleblower Protection Act offered still greater whistleblower protections for federal employees. It increased public awareness of the protections and accountability, and it mandated strict discipline for supervisors who retaliated against whistleblowers.

In recent years, whistleblowing has become a greater issue, both in government and in business. The Enron Corporation accounting scandal, bringing about the largest bankruptcy reorganization in US history at the time, came about because of a whistleblower in 2001. Executive Sherron Watkins revealed some of the irregularities in an in-house memo, though she was slow to actually go public.

During that period, we experienced a steady stream of whistleblowers. The following year, Cynthia Cooper, the Vice President of Internal Audit at the telecommunications company Worldcom (now MCI), uncovered about $3.8 billion in corporate fraud in company bookkeeping. Worldcom was the second-largest player in the long-distance phoning industry until Cooper's discovery, which brought about bankruptcy. Five executives went to prison.

But why do we call them "whistleblowers"? Probably because "tattletale" and "snitch" aren't the kind of positive labels that would encourage heroes to come forward. Ralph Nader, the activist and former presidential candidate, was one of the first to begin using the term regularly in the early seventies. But the idea of "blowing the whistle" is more than a hundred years old. Police once blew whistles to warn the public of a crime and to summon other officers. And of course, referees blow whistles in sporting events.

Today, a whistleblower is generally an ordinary citizen on the inside of some business or institution who speaks up to shed light on illegal or unethical activities. Our client Jane, the commodity trader from the previous chapter, exemplified the problems of hostile workplace conditions as well as discrimination. But she was also a whistleblower who was fired for coming forward with her revelations about the treatment of women in her organization.

So the subject of whistleblowing doesn't have to be the vast sums of money in the Enron or Worldcom cases, or the Ponzi schemes of fraudster Bernie Madoff; it doesn't have to be a political scandal, such as the Pentagon Papers or Watergate. Nor does it have to be a huge national story. The proverbial whistle can be blown on problems of any size. Local whistleblowers are often featured in regional news on news broadcasts.

THE RISKS

Clients come to me with obvious anxiety. They're upset about willful violations of OSHA safety rules, financial fraud, or sexual harassment—whatever they see going on. On the other hand, they're very concerned about the consequences of speaking out publicly. Is it really true that they're protected? How can they know for sure?

The worst thing any attorney could do would be to assure these clients they had nothing to worry about. We speak realistically to them. They *do* need to think hard about what they're doing, particularly if the stakes are high enough. But by the time they walk into our office, they've come to a point of saying, "I just can't watch this happen anymore. I need to say something, even if nobody else will." And what will it take to change things? For the company, being outed publicly, receiving terrible publicity that damages its prospects, or being threatened with a costly settlement just might be required.

We tell our clients we can never predict how the company will respond when challenged. In 2007, New York Knicks coach Isiah Thomas and the parent company of Madison Square Garden were sued by the team's senior vice president, Anucha Browne Sanders, for sexual harassment, hostile work conditions, and retaliation. She testified that she'd endured crude insults and unwanted sexual advances from Thomas. When she reported the incidents, she'd been fired, clearly in retaliation.

Ms. Browne Sanders won the trial. She emerged from the court and told the press, "What I did here, I did for every working woman in America. And that includes everyone who gets up and goes to work in the morning, everyone working in a corporate environment."[7] She was awarded eleven million dollars, to be paid between Thomas and the corporation.

But even as she was making that statement, Thomas was standing nearby, protesting that he was innocent, that this was a travesty of justice, and that he would appeal. Another individual, a player on the team, was also identified in the trial as harassing an intern in the organization, yet neither he nor Thomas showed contrition. The NBA and sports in general continued to have this kind of problem, despite the plaintiff's motives in bringing it to light.

So I counsel our clients that they can never tell what will happen. They may lose their positions, and the companies or organizations in question may not change at all. Some of them just consider court settlements to be part of the cost of doing business. Some simply don't care. I realize the motives for coming forward are (or should be) positive change and seeing the right thing done. But the client shouldn't measure success by how the wrongdoer responds and whether things are indeed cleaned up. That's simply out of their control.

Instead, success has to be about how the client benefits from the consequences. Can he or she live with the publicity that might result? Are they ready to lose their job? Is it

---

[7] Associated Press, "Jury Rules Thomas Harrassed Ex-Executive; MSG Owers Her $11.6M," ESPN, October 2, 2007, https://www.espn.com/nba/news/story?id=3046010.

likely that a large cash settlement would be worth the stress of going through this whistleblowing exercise? In other words, it could be that you, the victim, file suit; you prevail in court and win a settlement; but it changes nothing at all. At that point, you have to cut losses and let it go.

On the other hand, maybe, just maybe, you make a difference. You change the world, or at least your little corner of it. Reforms result. New regulations are written up at the company, and bad executives or workers are fired. Then you've done something very important. You've helped to eliminate something wrong that would have hurt other people.

My judgment is that all of these cases taken together would, on average, result in incremental change. Business is always motivated by profit. There's a constant battle against corruption in the workplace, and in a competitive economy, someone's always willing to bend the rules to get an advantage. Or perhaps it's just a matter of people with no moral compass getting into positions of authority. The whistleblowers of the world are at least some form of restraining force against these. Who knows how much worse things would be without them? It takes a lot of those people, and it takes plenty of courage in each case. After all, how many other waste and sewage plants took harder looks at themselves after James Bobreski's case prevailed? How many Ponzi schemes dried up after the Bernie Madoff scandal hit the headlines?

We can't know these answers, but we have to have faith that lighting a candle is better than cursing the darkness.

IS IT ACTIONABLE?

For the reasons I've explained, the decision to speak publicly can be more difficult than one might expect.

Sometimes there are X factors. During 2020–2021, the warehouse of a major American retail company had employees working on conveyor belts four stories high, but without safety harnesses. Welders worked with high-temp tools while surrounded by flammable materials. But nothing was done, and no one wanted to come forward for fear of retaliation. Without giving their names, some of these factory supervisors told reporters that supply chain and other COVID-19 problems played havoc with the shipping schedule, there weren't enough workers on hand due to the pandemic, and safety measures were ignored in the resulting chaos. A contractor said that those who did try to speak up were fired for holding up production. "Whistleblowing is not going to pay my bills," he said.[8]

---

8   Kristian Hernández, "COVID Underscores Lack of Whistleblower Protections," *Stateline* (blog), The Pew Charitable Trusts, February 14, 2022, https://www.pewtrusts.org/en/research-and-analysis/blogs/stateline/2022/02/14/covid-underscores-lack-of-whistleblower-protections.

WHISTLEBLOWING

The agencies who oversee safety concerns are understaffed too, and once a complaint is filed, it may not be investigated for years. What happens to the whistleblower during that time? Yet OSHA received more than 4,600 whistleblower complaints in fiscal 2021, doubling the usual average. This was simply more fallout from a terrible year. But it's an example of the hazards of the whistleblowing question. The problem itself is bad, and perhaps worth exposing. But the remedy may not be worth it.

We also have to look closely at the conduct. Sexual harassment is serious. Workers being placed in physical danger is serious. These things are also clearly illegal. But what about gray areas? Some questions are matters not of legality but of strong opinions. A company policy can be poor, and perhaps even unethical, but are laws being broken? In American business, lots of boundaries are pushed. The issues aren't always clear cut. So the first rule is that the behavior must be illegal.

Retaliation is a bit easier to pinpoint. Federal laws do not cover matters of score-settling. Lots of statutes have antiretaliation provisions, particularly at the federal level, and if you can show you reported something illegal, you were fired, and there's no other credible explanation for your firing, you could have a case. There are OSHA regulations, employee safety and health regulations, and Title VII and other employment protection statutes that should protect you from being fired for speaking out.

This kind of decision is difficult enough, and the stakes are high enough, that you should certainly consult an attorney to look into the merits of your case. Once the attorney has investigated your story, you can make a decision based on what's best for you. On the one hand, you may be exposed to a lot of criticism and poor treatment, and even if you can't be legally fired in retaliation, it may not be feasible for you to work at that company.

Nor can you predict how the court will respond to your case. But on the other hand, our country needs people courageous and willing enough to come forward and report practices that shouldn't be happening. Many beneficial changes in the world have come about because of one insistent voice that spoke out, regardless of consequences. It's simply best not to go into such a case blind of those consequences.

And sometimes it's simply best to get away from a bad situation. If you blow the whistle, as we've said, you probably don't have a long-term future at that company. I tell clients that the stress and anxiety of going through with a complaint is bad for your life but good for your case. Juries see that you've paid a price. And when it's all over, and you can make a fresh start, you may find that's the best thing that could have happened to you, all other factors considered. Because there are still plenty of businesses in this world that respect people, follow the rules, and do everything right, and unlike your old workplace, they serve as fine places to spend the best eight hours of your day.

CHAPTER 10

EXIT STRATEGY

OLD HENRY HAS BEEN WITH THE COMPANY FOR forty years—he worked his way up from the mail room. He can tell you all about the good old days. At the age of sixty-seven, he's about to take his retirement to enjoy his grandchildren and a little travel. The company is throwing him a nice party and giving him a gold watch.

Every now and then, something like that still happens. But not too often. According to the Bureau of Labor Statistics, if you're a typical worker, you'll be part of twelve different companies in the course of your career.[9] Some of those positions may end in firing. Sometimes it's because your company goes out of business. Otherwise we walk away by our own choosing, for any number of reasons. We're restless, unhappy, or something better has arisen.

Quitting can make for an awkward moment, depending on why and how you do it. As I discuss it with clients, I can't help but recall the big exit scene in the 1996 Cameron Crowe movie *Jerry Maguire*. It's hard to imagine going out in a greater blaze of goofiness than Jerry, played by Tom Cruise.

Jerry manages athletes for a large sports agency. He's suave, smooth as silk, and he looks—well, like Tom Cruise. But after he makes a wrong move that displeases the management, it punishes him. With injured pride, Jerry quickly decides he's out of there. But he doesn't exactly stop to think things through. Instead, he walks out into the main work area of his agency, crowded with busy workers, computers, and ringing phones. Everything comes to a halt as he announces, "Don't worry, I'm not gonna do what you all think I'm gonna do, which is just *flip out!*"

Of course, he sounds exactly like someone who is *flipping out*. He continues with a little speech about the dishonesty

---

9 "Frequently Asked Questions (FAQs)," U.S. Bureau of Labor Statistics, last updated January 2, 2020, https://www.bls.gov/bls/faqs.htm.

of the times as he scoops a guppy out of a fish tank to take with him, in a little baggy. He's taking the fish, along with anyone in the room who wants to come with him and embark on a new adventure. He says, "Who's coming with me besides—'Flipper' here?"

Silence. People simply gawk. One mesmerized young lady does stand up and say she'll join him. Jerry stands in the door and says, "We'll see you all again. Good night." Exit Jerry, the young lady, and the fish.

Most of us handle resignations a bit more gracefully than that, thank heavens. But we've all acted on impulse and lived to regret it. It's a lesson that must be learned the hard way: important moves require careful planning.

In our society, occupation is at the center of our identity. It's how we afford life financially; it's what we do with our most productive hours of the most productive days of our week; it's the relationships that make a difference in our future. It's also one of the greatest sources of stress and anxiety, and we might be tempted, in a weak moment, to bail out. Or we might simply be blinded by excitement about future prospects. But have we given good, organized thought to what comes next?

It's important to have a plan.

We're as mobile in our job history as we are in every other way these days. We might leave a position because we're unhappy with the job we have. It could be we've gotten another offer, and it appears to be something better. Maybe we want to start our own business, go to work with the competition, or simply pursue another line of work. Whatever the reason, leaving a job can be a much more sensitive proposition than we might think. It can feel like simply walking away to get a fresh start somewhere else. The old job is in the rearview mirror.

But it's actually a little more complicated than that. For one thing, we want to make sure we take the high road, which is always the best-paved road. Second, we don't want a negative moment now coming back to haunt us when future employers check our references. And third, our past associates may not be as firmly in the rearview mirror as we think. Your paths could cross again.

It's not prudent to make big decisions on the spur of the moment anyway. We need to take a reasonable period of time, no matter how impatient we may feel. We owe it to ourselves to think it through; talk about it with our loved ones; thoroughly check out our options. So our best advice is to plan ahead, leaving as little as possible to chance. Once it's time to make the announcement, we'll be calm, cool, and collected, knowing that everything has been carefully prepared.

Let's consider three important words of caution, from a legal perspective.

BE HONEST

First, integrity becomes more crucial than ever during a transition. That includes being honest with yourself about your true prospects. If you want to own your own business, are you ready? Is it a realistic prospect?

If you want to look for another job, is the job market optimal at this moment? Can you find the kind of position you'd like without having to relocate? How do your spouse and children, if any, figure into this move?

It's possible to be so focused on work that we forget how many other things in life are *connected* to our employment. So we need to be honest with ourselves about this moment in time. A job change is no small matter.

Be honest also with your employer. Be as transparent as you possibly can. That is, don't leave the impression of having been deceptive, of sneaking around, furtively searching for other work while accepting your paycheck. If you can, be honest about your plans and the fact that you're at least considering moving on. It's true that in some places, that may be less feasible. The moment you express a desire to explore other opportunities, you'd be given the pink slip. Filter this and our other recommendations through your personal experience.

The point is, we should seek to be as transparent as we're allowed to be—which doesn't mean telling all that we know.

It's possible to let those around you know that you're leaving without going into great detail. If you're planning on going into direct competition with your current company, of course, it would be more than awkward to talk about that while you're still on the payroll.

As a matter of ethics, it's not a good idea to tell people you're going to a doctor's appointment when it's really a job interview. Or to visit your current clients with the motive of selling them on your new position. These things are certain to become evident, and they won't reflect well on your character.

So it's good to be honest and transparent. Just hold off on any announcements until you're really sure. Again, sleep on it, do your research, and be certain of your path, then be clear about your intentions—if it's at all possible to do that without causing a problem.

We find it easy to rationalize certain things. Management treated us poorly on some past occasion, so that justifies taking this sick day to go interview elsewhere. The problem is that, regardless of how you explain your grievances to yourself, it will be more difficult to explain them to someone else in the future. At some point it will become clear what you were up to, and you may get poor reviews when your character references are being checked.

I always counsel high integrity, of course. From beginning to end, our conduct should be as flawless as possible, because of simple right and wrong, because of consequences, because of legal issues. The lack of integrity in the world today makes that world a darker place. But in a period of transition, in leaving one position to move to another, it's important to be even more certain that our actions are beyond even the appearance of impropriety. These are the times when more eyes are on us—from companies past and companies future. In our eagerness to begin a new phase, we shouldn't give in to the temptation to compromise our honesty.

UNDERSTAND YOUR OBLIGATIONS

Second, know exactly where you stand from a legal perspective. I've counseled men and women who had plenty of ideas about what the company owed them, but they hadn't thought much about what they actually owed the company. Look into securing a copy of any contractual agreements you have with the company. As we've discussed in a previous chapter, it's important to know what you've signed. It's far better to study them now than to have them used against you later, in court.

There may be restrictive covenants that affect how and where you can go. You may have a non-compete clause or a confidentiality agreement that restricts what you can do with the knowledge you bring away from that business. If you have a copy of such an agreement, have an attorney review it. You can work through just about anything you may find in a restrictive covenant. If there's a non-compete clause, for example, it may be possible to negotiate that, if you're willing to give up certain things. But if you acted without knowing about these clauses, or you simply refused to take them into consideration, there could be trouble. You'd be legally liable and embroiled in a possible lawsuit.

We've also discussed arbitration. Many companies have employees sign an agreement to arbitrate rather than go through the courts. For a number of reasons, this could affect any disagreements you and your employer may have. Also, your freedom of movement could be restricted. The clause might contain the requirement that if you're sued for violating a non-compete clause, the arbitration would occur at the location of the company's home office, which could be thousands of miles from where you are. You'd be at a great disadvantage. That's one among a number of issues that come up with arbitration. So know your obligations in that regard.

Review your stock options. Have you been involved in an ESOP plan? This type of arrangement allows employees to participate with a financial interest in the company. If you leave, your interest may be paid out in both cash and stock, but you'll want to know exactly how your ESOP is set up. There could be other financial plans as well.

How will your benefits vest? They may vest immediately, or they may be spread out over as many as seven years. Your plan's vesting schedule might even become a reason to stay where you are. If you're close to becoming fully vested, the company's financial obligations increase. Know the difference between a cliff vesting plan (in which you become eligible for full pension at a specified date) and a gradual vesting plan. These details make a difference.

It's important to have copies of all the contracts, agreements, and arrangements you have with the company. Sometimes it can be frustrating trying to pull them all together, but you and an attorney need to know the precise details, and you really need to know them while you're making your future plans—not after the fact. Then again, requesting all these documents out of the blue can bring unwanted scrutiny if you're not able to be fully transparent about your intentions. Human Resources tends to raise an eyebrow when someone comes in and wants to see all employment agreements. It's one of the tip-offs that we're "looking around."

If you have rather simple employment arrangements, you may be able to make a fairly clean break and to do that on a positive note. These days, of course, executives in the higher reaches of management are more likely to have complex arrangements that have been negotiated during the period of hiring. Some of them are incentives or penalties specifically designed to make it more difficult to leave. So we need to have all the facts straight.

There's also the obligation known as the duty of loyalty. This is the principle that directors and officers of a corporation, through all decisions, must act without personal economic conflict. The duty of loyalty can be breached either by making a self-interested transaction or taking a corporate opportunity for ourselves. Competing with your employer while still on the payroll is a violation of the duty of loyalty. *Preparing* to compete is not, but it quickly becomes a gray area. There's a fine line between those two statuses. When does preparation become actual competition?

An example would be visiting a customer while you're still on the old payroll and saying, "I wanted to give you a heads-up that I'm leaving. But can I call on you in the future and count on your business at my new company?" In this instance, you've crossed the line into competing while still employed, and that's a violation of the duty of loyalty.

Many employees come to regret their use of company assets, including time, equipment, or communication channels, for personal interests. Let's say the company sends you to a conference or seminar regarding your field of business. At the time, you happen to be making future employment plans, and you find yourself networking for what's down the road. This will come to light quite easily, and you'll regret your carelessness in doing it on company time rather than your own.

The rule of thumb is that once you begin to make plans to leave for whatever reason, draw a strong line between your current employment and what you have planned in the future. Our hearts are set at another place, in the future, but our bodies and our commitments are to this place, in the present. It's a time to be careful. Keep the two businesses carefully compartmentalized so that you're fully loyal to your business as long as you're with that business. On your own time, plan your future. Make your transition as orderly, honest, and pleasant as possible.

TIME YOUR ACTIONS

My final word of advice once again has to do with careful planning. As a matter of fact, planning is this chapter's supreme takeaway. Never let circumstances dictate your actions. Plan ahead because circumstances are completely unpredictable. The only thing that mitigates their chaos in our lives is when we create margins, whether of time or resources.

For example, you might give a letter of two weeks' notice or thirty days' notice to your employer. Just go ahead and assume, for safety, that they reject the period of time you've specified. You're willing to stay two more weeks. You make it clear that you're happy to train a replacement and help tie up loose ends. But in many cases, the employer simply doesn't want you around once you've indicated your intention to leave. Your boss will say, "Please go ahead and leave now."

Management doesn't want the influence of someone no longer loyal to the team, or it's worried about espionage. It might be that you're seen as a possible recruiter of people from your current group. Or you might be looked upon as a traitor who is a bad influence. In some instances, it's a bit like a marriage after divorce papers have been served, and one of the parties has found somebody else. Things are awkward and perhaps unhealthy.

This is why you shouldn't count on that last paycheck or two. Plan as if it's already a lost cause. Be sure your financial situation is stable and your savings allow six to twelve months' worth of living expenses before you leave employment to start something new. As I've said: circumstances are unpredictable. Some of us knew people who were laid off just before the recent pandemic or who were in transition. No one could have guessed the ups and downs of the global economy in recent times.

Expect the unexpected. It's more than Jerry McGuire did at the beginning of his movie. If he'd followed the advice of this chapter, his new sports agency might have blossomed much more rapidly. He would have saved a lot of lost income. But it wouldn't have made for nearly as entertaining a film.

During your next transition, here's hoping you accentuate planning and orderly transition rather than a good laugh.

CHAPTER 11

NON-COMPETE AGREEMENTS & RESTRICTIVE COVENANTS

NON-COMPETE AGREEMENTS WERE ONCE ASSOciated with higher-level executives. In recent years, they've grown much more common so that these contractual restrictions are now asserted in all kinds of businesses and at every level. Some experts see them as one more factor restricting job mobility and therefore depressing wage increases. The opportunity to leave and compete is one of the factors traditionally used to gain a higher salary. Yet even in California, where non-competes are unenforceable, these agreements are keeping workers tied to their present positions.

That's why the president of the United States recently called on the Federal Trade Commission to look into curbing the proliferation of non-competes. After all, janitors, baristas, and entry-level factory workers are being asked to sign them now. One custodian protested, "I don't know any secrets!"[10] It's hard to imagine how he might "compete" with his current cleaning position at another facility. But he'll certainly know that if he wants to keep doing that kind of work, he can only do it at his current workplace.

The Economic Policy Institute contacted a large number of private sector business interests across America on this topic. It found that roughly half of respondents affirmed that non-compete agreements were used for some employees in their companies. Nearly a third said that **all** their employees were required to sign such an agreement, regardless of job position.[11] So it's

---

10 Lauren Weber, "The Noncompete Clause Gets a Closer Look," *Wall Street Journal*, July 21, 2021, https://www.wsj.com/articles/the-noncompete-clause-gets-a-closer-look-11626872430.
11 Alexander J.S. Colvin and Heidi Shierholz, "Noncompete Agreements," Economic Policy Institute, December 10, 2019, https://www.epi.org/publication/noncompete-agreements/.

important for all of us in the workforce to understand these contractual agreements and how to handle them.

Non-competes are just one of three types of restrictive covenants, which are employment agreements that limit the signee's actions during the period of the contract. This first category is the most common of the three, and the basic idea is: we will hire you and pay you the amount on this contract, and in exchange, you'll perform your duties, along with promising not to compete with this employer for this much time and throughout this specific area. The time period and the geography are then defined. Thus we'll bring you in and teach you everything we at (let's say) JKL Pies know about baking delicious pies, but you must first agree not to turn this teaching against us later. So essentially, you come to work for JKL, and if you choose to leave, it will be in another line of business because for perhaps two to five years, you can't be involved with baking in this part of the country.

The second type of restrictive covenant is the **non-disclosure agreement**. This one limits communication. It says, we will hire you at JKL Pies, but you are agreeing not to disclose business secrets, trade secrets, proprietary processes, or other information related to our business. Thus you can't use or share our baking methods. You can't reuse or reveal our recipes or our sources of ingredients. And also, hands off our customer list.

Again, there will be a time frame specified as well as a defined geographical region. Employees learn tradecraft—baking, real estate, machine operation, insurance, whatever—at a job. But with a non-disclosure agreement, leaving means walking away from what they've learned about that trade. It's good business for the company that must protect what's most valuable to it: its secrets and its information. For the employee, it can become a severe limitation that wasn't considered at the time of contract signing.

The third type of restrictive covenant is the **non-solicitation agreement.** This one is about marketing and hiring. The pie company will hire you, but you can't solicit our employees or customers in the future. That network of business relationships you build over the years at JKL will only serve you *at* JKL. Again, you walk away from them if you leave this job.

There's overlap among these three restrictive covenants, and your contract may contain all three or some combination of them. They all have the same aim of protecting a company's intellectual property. Otherwise, from the corporate perspective, you could get a job at JKL Pies, learn all the customers and suppliers, memorize the recipes, and set yourself up in competition after a year or two. In a highly competitive economy, it's no wonder so many companies are now using restrictive covenants at every level of business. They're also spending greater sums of money to develop the relationships, processes, and systems that define their companies. Those things become more valuable and require deeper protection.

In the past, different states have had their own laws. So if JKL operated in a number of states, contracts might all have to be written in different ways. But now, there's much more consistency because most states have adopted some version of the Uniform Trade Secrets Act (1979). This act protects trade secrets and proprietary information from misappropriation by employees and standardizes the protections. Forty-eight states, the District of Columbia, Puerto Rico, and the Virgin Islands have all signed on.

HOW MUCH IS "SECRET"?

Imagine you leave your position at JKL Pies, and you end up in a contract dispute concerning information you feel you can continue to use. Your position is that you haven't misappropriated any trade secrets. JKL disagrees. So how do you determine what is and isn't a secret?

Trade secrets are intellectual property and include formulas, practices, processes, designs, instruments, patterns, or compilations of information not readily known by the general public or by competitors. But they must be unique to the company and very well developed. JKL Pies can't claim the use of sugar as proprietary, but a complex formula for pie fillings might qualify.

Companies sometimes point to "trade secrets" that don't actually fill the requirements of the definition. But in a non-disclosure agreement, nearly anything can be treated as confidential, simply because it's labeled that way.

To enforce a non-disclosure agreement, your business needs a compelling business interest to assert. The classic one is a list of customer contacts. Everyone understands the reliance of a business on that database. A judge will be very protective of a company's customers and, in some cases, potential customers. Often employees will come to feel that these were *their* customers. In other words, "The procurement department people at MNO Food Distributors all know and trust me. I'm the one who built and cultivated that relationship! I've spent many hours with the head buyer; she doesn't know anyone else at our company. So why should I give that up?"

But if you've been under salary with your company, you've been paid, and you were performing your duties at all times in working with this customer, the judge will see the customer as company property.

But what if we're talking about a customer you didn't personally work with? In other words, JKL may have sold their pies to this chain of restaurants, but if so, it was through other salespeople. Then you could make a case that this chain was fair game. You wouldn't have an unfair advantage there, because you didn't build a relationship on company time; you didn't have a relationship at all. So JKL Pies is likely to assert that you're violating your contract, but they're less likely to prevail. What I call "ordinary competition" can't be limited unless there's an extremely compelling business interest.

On the other hand, what if you happen to know something unique about this chain of restaurants where you'd like to sell baked products from your new business? You don't know anyone there, but you have important information about that chain from your work at JKL. The salesperson assigned to that client told you. Perhaps it's about the pricing structure. You could come in with a business offer undercutting that pricing structure because you had inside information.

In that case, the judge is likely to find in favor of JKL. You'd be ordered to back away from business there because you had an unfair advantage. The important question would be, is pricing information something inherent in the marketplace, that any interested salesperson would already know, or is it truly rare and valuable information that gives a competitive advantage? The latter is probably true in this case.

PROTECT YOUR SECRETS

As non-compete agreements have grown more common, we've seen more situations in which a highly placed executive decides such an agreement is needed for every worker.

The company then spends a lot of time and money developing these agreements and seeing that everyone signs them. They've been told by their legal department they'll gain blanket protection for their confidential information.

It's certainly a start, but the company still has an obligation to spell things out. It needs to train its employees on the use and protection of its confidential information. Even more basic, it needs to carefully and specifically identify what is and is not their confidential information. So many times, I've spoken with CEOs or COOs and asked that question: "Can you identify your company's confidential information?" Then I find he or she can't do it. Certainly if the top executives aren't sure what the information is, employees can't be expected to know. But if there's a carefully defined set of essential company information, and everyone is briefed and reviewed on it, disputes are less likely later.

I once represented a Fortune 500 company that had a non-compete enforcement council. Serving that council, I traveled across the country seeing that non-competes were being followed. In one instance, I was helping a client prepare to testify at an injunction hearing on the following morning. The defendants in that case were two salespeople who'd left the company and taken a large chunk of its business with them. My clients had a very sophisticated customer service record that contained all kinds of specific information about their clients.

NON-COMPETE AGREEMENTS

Obviously it was invaluable data for the company. The suspicion was that these salespeople who'd left were still using the proprietary information. That was the basis of this non-compete issue.

The customer information database was password-protected, even from some in the company. You had to have special privileges to access it. All of this was by the book, just how such things should be handled. But as we were about to finish our evening's work, I went into the company lobby to use the receptionist's phone. My glance fell upon a computer printout. This was in the days of dot-matrix printing and extra-large, green-and-white-striped printer paper. At the top, I saw the words "Customer List." I picked it up, paged through it, and realized this was almost certainly the very customer record that was being contested. Not only had it been printed out and placed on a desk—it had been placed on the *reception desk*, which is a high-traffic area in any company. Anyone could have walked in, picked it up, and left with it.

The receptionist, whom we'll call Debbie, was present. I asked her what kind of report I had in my hands. She said, "Oh, I'm not supposed to have that! But the sales manager got tired of answering questions when the salesmen were in the field. So he printed this out for me so I could handle the questions myself. It saves time for the sales manager."

So much for confidentiality. If the company couldn't protect its information better than that, then it couldn't complain about the information escaping. As it happened, we resolved the case before the hearing. If we hadn't, I think the carelessness of protecting this list could have been used against us. The salespeople who'd left would have known exactly how poorly the information was concealed from prying eyes.

What defines a secret? How well it's kept. Once it circulates, it loses its value.

DON'T GET CUTE

I've also counseled a number of people who were determined to violate non-compete agreements. This happens a lot. Perhaps they have legitimate reasons for going in this direction. Maybe they don't, and they're fooling themselves. Or maybe they're angry at how they were treated, and what they want is revenge on the company they've left. Whatever the reason, sometimes they try to get cute. And that's a big mistake.

There are very few loopholes in non-compete enforcement. Again, judges respect the written word on a signed contract. They look at what is spelled out and legally binding. If you skirt an obligation from a contract by trying to hide behind a technicality, a judge is going to catch on quickly. This is the whole point of the court's equitable power: the ability to overlook what might be technical compliance when it doesn't live up to the spirit of the law in your obligation.

NON-COMPETE AGREEMENTS

I had a client, a company that bought someone's business in Arkansas. The company they bought sold insurance, and a man and his wife had built it from the ground up. The couple stayed on, but somehow the man never quite accepted that he was no longer the owner and no longer called all the shots. Inevitably, he had a falling out with the parent company. He turned in his resignation and started a brand-new, competing business. But he felt he had beaten the non-compete—his *wife* was running this new company. Clearly, he was behind the scenes giving direction, of course, but in his mind, he was technically following the old contract: he wasn't competing; his wife was. Let them prove he was the one pulling the strings.

The problem with that was fingerprints. Our actions, particularly in business, leave lots of fingerprints. His customers were brought in, old and new, and gave testimony of their dealings with his businesses. It quickly became clear that his wife was a wonderful person whom everyone liked, but she wasn't an insurance executive. She was an administrator who kept the books and ran the office, but she didn't know the trade. He was performing all the functions he had in the past.

The trial took two days. The federal judge finally said, "Sir, you can put lipstick on a pig, put a dress on it, and call it a petunia, but it's still a pig."

Not only is it a pig, but you don't need to be too sharp-eyed to be able to see it. That's the way it is when we try to avoid contractual requirements by looking for loopholes or technicalities. They work much better in our imagination than they do in a courtroom. We think of contracts as offering the strict letter of the law, and they do. But we often forget that judges also attend to the spirit of the law. They understand why these regulations are written in the first place, and they protect those principles.

NOTHING PERSONAL— IT'S JUST BUSINESS

I also counsel people to be very careful about the desire for revenge. All of us come out of a job at some point a little bruised emotionally, and there's a natural desire to get even. Two different people could carry out the same action, one in good faith and the other with the intent to harm. Take them both to court, and the outcomes will be different because the judge sees and understands the motives. They can't really be hidden. My word of advice is that the best revenge is to live well, prosper, and stay out of court.

Cases involving non-competes and restrictive agreements tend to settle, at the end of the day. This is business litigation. Our emotions get involved, but when the time comes, we need to realize that as personal as it may feel, it's ultimately business, and we need to view it through that lens and make our decisions based on the best business strategy, not our gut-level emotions.

From the vantage point of the company, for example, it's easy to act out of the fog of war. Someone leaves, and a week later, a key customer is lost. Management jumps to the conclusion that these two events are related—why, that snake is stealing our business, robbing us of our clients! Yet it's possible that's not the case; the two things may not be related. Still, the company fires a shot across the bow through threatening letters then lawsuits. It's an emotional response, and it may be totally unnecessary.

Maybe the two things *are* connected—the employee has, in fact, stolen that customer. Even then, someone needs to look at the situation with cold objectivity and ask the question, how badly is this really hurting us? There's always a business solution that would ultimately be far less costly than going to war in the legal system. Business is negotiation, give and take. Make a deal based on the business interests of each side. It's been said, never go to court on principle, and there's truth to that.

One of my clients had a father who owned a business as a mechanic in rural Missouri, specializing in farm equipment. Over time, he'd developed a large network of farmers and others with heavy equipment. He maintained fleets of tractors, combines, and other machines. My client grew up in that business, and his father had taught him the ins and outs of the mechanical world and introduced him to all the customers. This business controlled about eight million dollars' worth of revenue per year, and the father was receiving sizable commissions on that money.

But one day, a good deal came along. He sold his business to a national company, which hired the young man as his father was now retiring.

For a time, the young man did well. He had signed a non-compete agreement as part of his employment contract, and it restricted him from doing that kind of business in the state of Missouri. There was also a non-solicitation clause that restricted him from soliciting any of the customers if he left.

Over the course of a year or two, the young man began to quarrel with his new management. The whole style of business was different from the small-business model the father and son had followed. They wanted a more corporate personality, less time spent catering to existing customers, and that type of thing. There was a competitor not too many miles away, and the son was friends with the managers there. As he described his conflicts to them, an invitation was forthcoming: come work with us, and bring your business with you. He did just that.

A lawsuit followed, of course, and it was emotional and hotly contested. I represented the young man, and other attorneys took the other side. We all took stock of the situation. It became clear that no matter who won, if they failed to make a deal, both sides would lose most of their business. It was a classic no-win situation either way. So the two interests managed to put their respective anger issues aside, sit down, and do some horse trading. The young man walked away with about six million dollars of the eight million he'd had. It wasn't everything, but it was plenty, and cutting his losses made sense. Based on saving those commissions, he was able to set up a new business, and the last I talked to him, he was looking toward a bright future with the past bumps in the road completely behind him.

The message of this story is clear. Business is hardball. Those who play the game can get hurt and build grudges. Everything in our human nature urges us to hit back. But doing so almost always works against all the principles of business, which is about numbers, losses, gains. When you go to court in these cases, the witnesses will be customers, suppliers, and other business relationships whose last desire is to get involved in acrimony. And rather than investing in new products, new personnel, and new ideas, you're investing in legal advice, which really isn't an investment at all. It's a money pit, and it's the least profitable activity a business can engage in. There are times when there's no alternative, but most of the time, a business solution is superior to a legal one.

Smart executives write and enforce their contracts carefully. They identify their intellectual property and important information and educate their employees on them. And they stay out of court as much as possible, so they can be as *profitable* as possible.

Smart employees similarly think carefully before they make major moves, and they leave the past behind them. Getting even, if it even happens, is a poor substitute for getting on with the promise of the future. Restrictive covenants can be burdensome, but the worst restrictions might well be the ones we place on ourselves.

All of that said; Nothing is more personal than business.

CHAPTER 12

BEST HIRING PRACTICES

Accoring to a BBC story, George (as we'll call him) had all the necessary credentials. He could write computer code in several languages. He was so quiet, you hardly knew he was there. He was productive, and he was smart—perhaps a little too smart, as it turned out.

The company, like many, had been moving toward expanded telecommuting. More and more frequently, developers were encouraged to work from home, where they might get large workloads done in their own informal surroundings. Managers would monitor their output, so there was no fear of loafing. The company set up a virtual private network (VPN) to allow personnel to have access to all their work resources.

But after a while, there were security concerns. There seemed to be a huge amount of data traffic between the company and China. This made no sense, but the great fear was that Chinese hackers were stealing confidential information. Yet it all connected to George's terminal; no one else's machine was compromised. When the security people investigated further, they began to find dozens of PDF files, which turned out to be invoices from Chinese workers.

It turned out George had been outsourcing his daily work to China. He had managed to get all his assignments done for the cost of about one fifth of his salary. He always turned in his work early too. George simply made assignments, paid the invoices, then spent the rest of his time watching cat videos on YouTube and monitoring his auction bids on eBay, as the auditors discovered. He had no interest in espionage, but he was really into humorous feline antics.

But it was worse than that. Once the entire investigation was completed, the company had to alert a whole string of other companies. George was taking on work for those companies too. Why limit himself to one scam? He was making hundreds of thousands of dollars annually at a cost of only fifty thousand bucks paid to his subcontractors.

Needless to say, his pink slip was forthcoming.[12]

Hiring new employees can be a sketchy business. We see only what interviewees want us to see. We hear earnest, carefully rehearsed answers to our stale questions. The prospective candidate résumés may or may not be completely candid. When we ask them to name a personal flaw, they tell us they just work too darn hard. We try to interview a reasonable number of candidates and make the best selection, relying on subjective impressions as much as job credentials. And with any luck, the employee will last the 4.1 years that is the average shelf life of American employment in one company.[13]

By the way, let's look at some other measures. How long does it take for a company to move through the whole interview process? About twenty-four days. How much does it cost? Around $4,500 per employee. And what about turnover? How much does that cost? Apparently, one-third of an employee's annual salary, once we hire his or her replacement.[14] So every $45,000 worker you hire really costs you $60,000 that first year.

---

12 "US Employee 'Outsourced Job to China'," BBC, January 16, 2013, https://www.bbc.com/news/technology-21043693.

13 Bureau of Labor Statistics, U.S. Department of Labor, "Employee Tenure in 2022," news release USDL-22-1894, September 22, 2022, https://www.bls.gov/news.release/pdf/tenure.pdf.

14 "10 Hiring Best Practices and Lessons," *Wharton Online Insights* (blog), The Wharton School, University of Pennsylvania, May 7, 2019, https://online.wharton.upenn.edu/blog/10-hiring-best-practices-and-lessons/.

You do the math. Those are average numbers, but when it comes to hiring for our businesses, we need to be better than average. We need to be excellent because beyond the time loss and financial costs, our companies will rise and fall depending on the quality of our hires.

THE FUNDAMENTAL THINGS

During our times, we've seen periods of high unemployment, when jobs simply weren't available. Good positions were highly competitive, and it was a buyer's market for employers, who could afford to be exceedingly choosy and extremely cheap. We've also seen almost the opposite—periods of low unemployment and companies with crises of labor shortages, driving up desperation and remuneration. Recently there has been talk of a "skills gap," with a shortage of employees who had the right training and skills for the work needed. Companies have had to invest more in recruiting and active interviewing, as opposed to the passive methods in the past (advertising openings, accepting résumés, granting single interviews, and making the selection).

Companies today are competing for talent, so they find themselves striving to make their organizations more attractive to prospective employees. They might offer in-house childcare or allow more employees to work from home, if that's what the more talented sector of the workforce desires. Better benefits, of course, make a difference. Diversity and inclusion are quickly becoming more important in the hiring picture, and of course recruiting is becoming more data-driven, since those tools are much more readily available than in the past. It's a fact that much more information on candidates is available so that, among other things, social media is out there to be reviewed for most interviewees. The self-portrait painted through social media may stand in contrast to what comes through on the résumé. Experience and credentials are shown in glossy form on the resume; character and personality come through in social media.

All these items are high-level trends, and they make sense. But in this final chapter, I'd like to offer a more personal perspective on best hiring practices, based on my observations from working with very different companies through time. Some are small businesses, some Fortune 500. Some are well run, and some are in chaos. Some are traditional in every way, while others are on the cutting edge of new ideas and trends. Whatever the case may be with any of these companies, I've come to believe that, as the old song says, "the fundamental things apply as time goes by." Some principles never change.

First, I believe that good hiring starts with accurate job descriptions and the understanding on both sides of what this job is and what lights up the scoreboard. In other words, what does it take to "score" in this position? Along with my work with CEOs and managers, I also talk to management consultants, and they place a great stress here. You're interviewing for this particular position. Exactly what are its parameters? Where do its responsibilities begin, and precisely where do they end? How does this position fit within the overall framework of the company? How does the management hierarchy flow through it, so that we don't have someone receiving conflicting signals from two different directions?

I shouldn't have to say this, but it begins with management. If the leaders can't answer these questions, they'll never be able to hire employees that can. The truth is, most companies get so involved in handling challenges, moving forward, putting out fires, and dealing with the gifts and limitations of personnel that the job descriptions grow rather hazy. This person began with this job, but it evolved into something else, out of immediate necessity or because this particular worker had these other gifts. A company structure that isn't carefully managed is like a lawn and garden that are neglected. Things overgrow, things die, and weeds sprout here and there, ultimately threatening the whole property.

This is why I've advised maintaining your garden: job descriptions and structure should be reviewed quarterly if possible, or at least annually, instead of every five years or whenever things finally fall apart. It's amazing how many problems can be solved if we simply clarify who's supposed to be doing what. Job descriptions must be clearly understood, then, by those doing the hiring. Then they must be explained in plain, clear language to those applying for the job.

As you revisit job descriptions, evaluate the numbers. Do we need this number of workers in this department? Should we have fewer here and more over in that other department? What's the most efficient balance? A lot of companies are unruly in being overstaffed in one place and understaffed in another.

Give attention to how you word these job descriptions, for the benefit of your company and for the benefit of your applicants. For some reason, we often use vague, confusing, and unnecessary language in our job descriptions. They should not sound like legalese (a language I know too well). And, though they should be specific and complete, they shouldn't be too lengthy. Keep them on a sixth-grade reading level. Writing a poor job description hampers the work of recruiters, if you use them, and also keeps some of the best applicants from applying. If they're not sure what this job is, they'll skip over it.

Compensation is a similar issue. How much value is this position to the company? Sometimes we think of our jobs politically rather than functionally. Someone may be low on the totem pole, but their work may be critical to the company's success. We've all read about CEOs with multimillion-dollar salaries who offer inadequate benefits to their people. If there's particularly high value, pay accordingly. And again, you'll need to revisit compensation scales regularly. Where are salaries too low? Where are they too high? Processes, systems, and practices change.

Qualifications need a careful look. Are we hiring people who come in with sufficient abilities? Full training requires time and money. Be sure job descriptions are written and interviews are done in such a way that you're hiring people who have already been there and done that. Entry-level positions, of course, are the exception; that's why they're called "entry level."

CULTURE AND COMPOSITION

With all these angles and all these requirements in finding just the right person with the right abilities who has the right job description and will be given the right compensation, it takes special effort to find the right kind of people—that is, in terms of character and chemistry with future team members. I believe it's important to keep a close eye on specific qualifications, but we have to realize that it's often personality issues that shorten the length of employment. If you need a computer programmer, and you find one who's excellent, it will do you little good if he can't get along with others in the office—just as the best all-around person isn't always the best for a particular job.

Thus we need to think about company culture, build that culture, understand it, and hire in accordance with it. What are the key values in your company? What are the essential attitudes all employees must have? Part of company culture can be designed, spelled out, taught, and nurtured in your company. Some is just a "feel," something intangible that says, "This is a fun place to work. We enjoy functioning as a team and getting great things done." Managers have to be out and around, getting that feel for things, understanding the collective personality of the group, and then interviewing and hiring to complement rather than clash. Anyone making a hiring decision for a department had better know that department quite well.

Meanwhile, diversity is important, and it takes a great deal of effort to encourage it. Why is it important that we have a balance of genders, that we represent racial backgrounds and life experiences? Wouldn't that work against the perfect chemistry we're seeking? Not at all. Again, it takes great effort to find just the right people, while maintaining a healthy, diverse workforce. But there are hidden benefits. Creativity surges when the team isn't cookie-cutter homogeneous. Different life experiences bring in different outlooks. Clients are better understood when your team is more representative, when it "looks like America" and also reflects your customer base.

I'm not talking about hiring someone because of color or creed and ignoring qualifications. You're still looking for the best people to get the job done. But all things being equal, you're always taking into consideration the kind of diversity you want your office to represent. There are legal requirements these days, but we're not motivated by those. We're motivated by the fact that hiring for diversity is good business. I've always approached legal requirements by asking, "How can I turn this into a business advantage?"

You'll have to broaden your search locations. Go outside your usual channels to search for talent. Be certain you're looking in historically Black colleges and universities as well as state schools. LinkedIn networking groups for women might offer good leads. You can check religious groups of various kinds. And if you look in all of these, you'll have a diverse pool of applicants. It simply requires being proactive and intentional. This isn't about fulfilling quotas; it's about building a stronger and more capable pool of talent by having a variety of outlooks and backgrounds.

A CONSTANT FUNNEL

How recently have you reviewed your application methods and interview processes? Testing is growing more popular. We have a number of "old reliable" personality tests to show how people fit in. Newer tools such as Gallup's "StrengthsFinder" are popular. Then there are particular tests to measure aptitude or readiness in various fields.

I recommend testing "blindly" in that you set criteria ahead of time, to eliminate subjectivity and make sure you're taking a hard look at aptitude level, with no bias. For example, you might decide you'll require a specific score on this kind of test for anyone you hire. The candidate you might tend to favor may not have reached that score. Deciding criteria beforehand creates objectivity. Most of the time we're not even aware of the various biases that cloud our judgment.

Given the turnover margin we see in companies today, it's important to have recruiting as an ongoing procedure, not an "as needed" one. Approach finding employees the same way you find customers. You're always on the lookout for potential customers. In the same way, you should keep an eye out for outstanding individuals who would make a positive difference in your company. I think of it as a funnel into which you're constantly pouring new candidates. You sift through them, find the one or two best among them, and bring them through the spout into your hiring process.

The more thorough your search, the more thoughtful and well conducted your hiring process, the more you're going to improve your company. I'm always amazed to see companies who view hiring as a necessary evil and give it low priority. We are who we hire. We will rise and fall by the quality of the people we bring into our operation. And speaking as an attorney, I'll say that the companies who do the best hiring, who educate those employees the best, and who create the strongest cultures spend the least time in court.

Think about the example of college athletics. Every good athletic director has a confidential file with three or four names of coaches he'd like to hire for a particular sport—even though the job is currently filled. Some scandal could suddenly erupt with the present coach, or the program could fail, and the coach would need to be replaced. Or the coach could be hired away by another program. So if the athletic director waits until he has a vacancy to think about replacements, he will find himself under a great deal of pressure to hire someone quickly. After all, team recruiting never stops. Rival coaches are out there taking the best athletes, and they won't go somewhere that is between coaches. And at any given time, there's serious competition for the most successful coaches.

So the athletic director must be ahead of the game. He must be ready to act quickly and decisively when the moment comes to find his candidate. And what happens if he has to make a subpar hire in desperation? The program withers. Boosters become upset. Eventually, another transition may cost the program millions of dollars.

The world of business really isn't much different. Today, we need to be fast and effective. There should be an active pool of viable candidates, even when there aren't openings. We need the best people, and we need to find, train, and deploy them as quickly as possible. If we fail to do that, next time, we may find ourselves sitting at the other end of the interview table.

ABOUT THE AUTHOR

Alan Crone is the Chief Executive and Founder of The Crone Law Firm. Crone represents employees, executives, and entrepreneurs in legal matters that affect their ability to "bring home the bacon." Whether he's helping achieve a business dream or seeking compensation for someone who's been treated unfairly, he draws from a deep well of compassion and experience. He's a master at devising winning strategies and innovative tactics.

Alan is a graduate of Memphis State University. A fifth-generation Memphian, he is a voracious reader and semi-avid golfer. He has been active in local and state politics for decades and stays busy with community and church service as well as charitable work. He is the former head of the Shelby

County Republican Party, Chief Counsel for the Tennessee Department of Employment Security, a Member of the Memphis City Council, and Special Counsel to the Mayor of Memphis.

Alan is also the very proud father of three children and is devoted to his wife, Allison.

ACKNOWLEDGEMENTS

I want to thank God for all the good things he has given me, specifically here for my legal skills and career, and my tremendous team at the firm and my family. Special thanks goes to my wife Allison and my kids, James, Charlie, and Maggie for their support, love, and friendship. I also want to thank my friends Miles Mason and Mack Bradely who are the brothers I never had. My actual sibling and co-worker Alison "Maggie" Crone is the real reason the Crone Law Firm does so well. Her warmth, love, and care for each client and member of our team is the glue which holds us together and the fuel which propels us to new heights. I would be nothing without my parents, Jim and Dottie Crone. They are always supportive and gave me everything I needed to succeed. An example of love and sacrifice, the best education, and my love of Jesus. They opened the wide world of art, literature, and intellect at a young age to my sister and me. I love you all. Thank you.